POWER OF
FORGIVENESS

POWER OF FORGIVENESS

PRACTICING SELF-FORGIVENESS

BY

KURT GASSNER

My-mindguide.com

Power of Forgiveness
Kurt Gassner

Impressum
My-mindguide – The publishing trademarke of trendguide Capital
GmbH, Klenzestr. 42a, 80469 Munich, Germany.

Reg. Nr. HRB Munich 206639, VAT 152 123 159, CEO: Kurt
Friedrich Gassner
Web: www.my-mindguide.com, mail: gassner@my-mindguide.com

Paperback ISBN: 978-3-949978-12-8
Ebook ISBN: 978-3-949978-14-2
Hardback ISBN: 978-3-949978-13-5

PREFACE

When problems seem uncontrollable, quitting may look like the easiest way out. A word of encouragement when we fail is worth more than an hour of praise after success. Life doesn't always offer a soft landing. Everyone has a cross to carry. Some begin to believe that their cross may be heavier than others, but the truth is that our cross will shape us towards greatness. Our ability to achieve the conquest of our cross will likely predict our success in life.

One of the best ways to heal wounds is to learn from the situation and use these moments to focus on growth and momentum. If we get stuck thinking about what "should have been," we can freeze in painful feelings and memories. Forgiveness is essentially a positive way of acknowledging and letting go of negative thoughts and feelings. It is a skill, something that you improve over time. And you will get more and more benefits from doing so. Your personality improves to make it easier to be around you, but ultimately, you become happier as you become less and less bothered by other people's setbacks along the way. We hear this phrase all the time: "I want to be free." If you take the train off the track, it is free, but where does it go? The desire to write this book was born out of the need to heal from past pain with the power of forgiveness. This book is meant to serve as a practical guide and motivation to develop self-forgiveness and overcoming past life trauma.

I will share with you my own path of life and the way I escaped the vicious circle of guilt. How I was hurt and truly struggled with the concept of forgiveness. When you are born, and the perpetrators are named mom and dad, it's not easy to heal your inner wounds. But I did it, and I don't feel like a victim anymore. I see myself as a helper and, in this role, I want to help you to pass your own traumas.

This book proffers solutions to some of the issues of life experiences and healing, comprising of fifteen chapters that treat topics with the following themes:

- FORGIVE + HEAL
- I CAN NOW FULLY FORGIVE MY FATHER
- I CAN NOW FORGIVE MY Mother
- I CAN NOW FORGIVE MY SISTER
- I CAN NOW FORGIVE THE SECOND WIFE OF MY FATHER
- I CAN NOW FULLY FORGIVE MYSELF
- I CAN NOW FULLY FORGIVE MY EX-Business-PARTNER
- I CAN NOW FORGIVE ALL MY EX-PARTNERS
- I CAN EVEN FORGIVE MY TENANT
- THE VICIOUS RELATION OF PERPETRATOR-VICTIM
- THE TRIANGLE PERPETRATOR - VICTIM - HELPER
- THINK LIKE THE PERPETRATOR
- WHY WE SHOULD ESCAPE THE VICIOUS CIRCLE
- SELF-FORGIVENESS

Table of Contents

My-mindguide.com

FEAR MODEL

PrimTrigger/Adventures
Anger.
Anxiety.
Sadness
Pain
Feeling overwhelmed, vulnerable, abandoned,/out of control
Memories tied to a traumatic event.
Loneliness. Muscle tension
Negative Beliefs
I'm unlovable
I'm inadequate.
I'm weak.
I'm a failure.
I am not enough."
I'm pathetic.
Basic Fears
To be Alone
Not Enough
Loss of Control
Primal Fears
My-mindguide.com

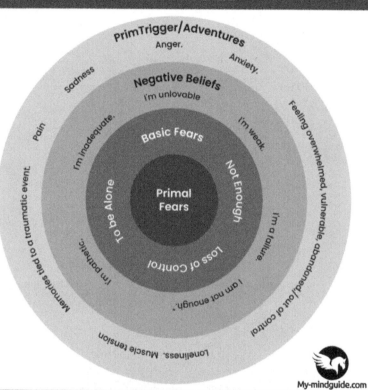

THE ICE MOUNTAIN
MIND MODEL

CONSCIOUS MIND
FACTS
Numbers, Foots, Logic

SUB CONSCIOUS MIND
RELATIONS
Instinct, Feeling, Desire, Traumata, Emotion

Chapter One

INTRODUCTION

When you are faced with a challenge, you probably have a handful of strategies to help you overcome it. Although your approach varies slightly from issue to issue, you probably handle most cases the same. Your personality could, for example, be a problem solver. When faced with a stressful event or challenge, you go straight to the source and work on it until you fix the problem or reduce your stress to a more manageable level. It's easy to focus on feelings of injustice or injustice when someone hurts you or does something wrong.

One thing that connects us as human beings is our ability to feel pain.

Whether this pain is physical or emotional, we all have been hurt. However, what separates us is how we deal with this pain. Experts have found that when emotional pain keeps you from recovering from a situation, it is a sign that you are not moving forward in a growth-oriented manner.

One of the best ways to heal wounds is to learn from the situation and focus on growth and momentum. If we get stuck thinking about what "should have been," we can freeze inside us painful feelings and memories.

However, there is nothing you can do to change the injury you sustained. In other words, the damage is done, and all you have to do is let it go and move on.

Forgiveness can help you rid yourself of the pain and begin to heal it. Of course, forgiveness is not always easy.

It may take a while for you to accept your pain before you feel able to forgive.
What if acting immediately isn't your thing? You can try to hack your emotions by looking at the situation from a different perspective or relying on those close to you.

The decision to forgive someone is a deliberate action to free yourself. You act with a sense of agency and purpose wholly intended to heal you. By ignoring your abuser, you can accept the circumstances that led to your abuse and can let go of your preoccupation with the past and move forward with a focus on yourself. Therefore, forgiveness is not about condoning their behavior. Nor is it about letting them back in so that they can abuse you again.

Certain things are fundamental to human fulfillment. If these basic needs aren't met, we feel empty, incomplete. We may try to fill the void through nonsense additions. Or we may become complacent, temporarily satisfied with partial fulfillment.

But whether or not we fully acknowledge or address these needs on a conscious level, we know they are there deep inside. And they are essential. We can validate them through our own experience. We can validate them through the experience of other people.

As understood in Western societies, especially modern Christian communities, forgiveness is a puzzle, and it is a concept that I have struggled with for many years. It is something so warm and fuzzy that it is a challenge to apply it to a situation that is as painful as violence or aggression. Impossible, I would have said.

So what forgiveness means is letting go, releasing the bad feelings you have towards the person who hurt you. Holding onto his pain is like never throwing out the trash, and bad feelings are like eggshells and coffee grounds and old cans and tissues that are harder to carry every day.

You may not be able to find the grace to do this for a long time. Working on it with an advisor is a great idea. I will explain later who really can help you on your journey and whom you can trust. Forgiving yourself is part of the job, too, and probably the hardest of all. It's worth it because you don't want to carry that person into your life longer than you already have. Learn the lesson, then let it go. Many people share your experience, and we are all on your side. There's a famous quote: "The weak can never forgive. Forgiveness is the exclusive domain of the strong." You see, no matter how they behave with you or how badly they have treated you, remember, we are all connected. In the spiritual tradition of the East, there is the strong belief that every person who comes into your life has a reason. You have a karmic account of past lives with them. And you can't even ignore that fact because, in the end, it's the truth. If you don't forgive them now, that account will never end. It will continue throughout your life, if not the next time you are born. Even if we, Westerners, don't adhere to that belief, we learned to pray, "Forgive us our debts as we forgive our debtors". It doesn't matter if you are saying: "Yes, I have my karmic account with you, and I'm fixing it right now, right here. I forgive you. I hope we don't hold a grudge later in life," and move on. Or you just shake hands, hug him or her and let all the grudge pass.

It's important to forgive so that you don't get twisted inside and unable to move on with your life. If you don't forgive, then you hate. There may be a perfectly valid reason for this to happen. One of the leading causes of hate is that someone has humiliated and hurt you. Another is fear.

Now, I want to share with you my own painful lessons of forgiving.

The Drama Triangle (Forgive the Past)

Wife and Husband

Helper
(Husband and Wife)

Forgiveness
(Mutual Therapy)

Forgiveness
(Mutual Therapy)

Husband
Perpetrator

Wife
Victim

Fight between Couple

My-mindguide.com

Chapter Two

I CAN NOW FULLY FORGIVE
MY FATHER

There are certain things your parents do that you wish you could have a say in. You want to do all you can to possibly change something about it, but in the end, you really couldn't do anything, maybe because you were a kid. But as you grew up, you realized that even if you weren't a kid, you wouldn't have been able to do anything about this. One of these situations that I found myself locked into was the divorce of my parents. I have always looked at my dad as my role model. There had always been this belief that guys look up to their dads when determining the kind of lifestyle they want to live. The same they say appears in the life of ladies; they tend to try to live the same life their moms are living. So, while growing up, I saw my dad as my role model; I did my best to be like him. My dad's marriage to my mom wasn't the kind of marriage that I would like to say was smooth; they had their issues, and some of the problems they had were too serious to be ignored, but they always found a way to patch things up.

I always looked at my dad as my role model until an incident changed everything I believed about him. I knew he wasn't perfect, but he was still family, and I loved him, but this issue that came up broke me. He was going to divorce my mom to be with another woman. At first, I thought it was a joke because I had never thought of him leaving my mom before then. The incident kind of destabilized me. I protested, but he didn't seem bothered about the whole thing.

My dad eventually divorced my mom to be with another woman. My issue wasn't that he divorced my mom to be with another woman; he abandoned his four kids, which included me. I didn't know someone could be this insensitive; it greatly affected how I saw him. I decided to stop seeing him as my role model. I was mad at him. I hated him; I told myself that I would never forgive him for divorcing my mom to live with another woman. Above all, I told myself I would never forgive him for abandoning us, his kids. For so many years, I hated him, I never wanted to see him, and when I did see him, I made sure our conversation was as brief as possible. I just didn't want to hang around him for too long.

I hated my dad for a very long time. He started reaching out more than he usually did, he would always do his best to make sure we met, but I always never wanted to meet him. As I grew up into a man, we never really got along well, but I saw things a bit differently from how I used to see something before. He divorced my mom because he couldn't continue living with her. I don't know if he tried working things out, but I did put myself in his shoes and concluded that a man has the right to seek a divorce, no matter the reason. However, I was still mad about how he abandoned us. He gave his second wife all she needed and ignored us. I was still bitter at him, but at some point, everything changed; I realized that we don't have all the time in the world to be on earth; we only have less than or barely more than a century to live. Since we don't have much time to live on earth, what are the benefits of not being at peace with those parts of your life? We're not on earth forever, but during the little moment we have to spend, how do we make it remarkable with those we love? These people we love, whom we are seeing now, time will come when we will not be able to see them again. After I thought about all these, I decided to forgive my dad. Despite all he did to us, despite how he abandoned us for his new wife, whom he probably saw as his only family at the time, I still found a way to forgive him.

I didn't just forgive my father for just him; I forgave him for me, too. I knew I would be in so much regret if anything went wrong with my dad, and I was yet to forgive him for what he did to us. I didn't want something that would end up ruining my life. I managed to see him in a different light in another time. I imagined how he was brought up, how he suffered when he was a little boy. My research brought up that his father abandoned him and his mother when he was just 6. He was forced to join the NAPOLA, the elite school of the NAZIS, when he was just 13. The military drill, the unhuman social environment should harden him. Strong like Krupp steel was the slogan in those times. I saw him crying, homesick and brainwashed. Then I met him in my imagination when he was 17 and forced to join the SS in the last days of Hitler's regime. How he lost his right leg – he, the best Sportsman in class. How he struggled to become a PHD in Chemistry. How he founded a family and got three children, and it was hard to meet month's end. I knew for sure he was a victim like me, and he was the perpetrator **and** the victim. So I could full heartily forgive him, which helped me heal. I had no peace of mind after I ignored him; he felt more accessible before me after I forgave him too. I stopped being a victim to the hate I had for my dad, and with time, everything balanced itself.

Now, I know that so many people like me have been hurt by their dad. I know how badly they are at seeing him. I had been there, but you have to forgive him no matter what. Your hate for him will continue to consume you if you don't do something about it. You have to forgive your dad and have the same peace of mind that I had moments after forgiving my dad. Remember that you might end up regretting it if you delay doing what's needed.

The Drama Triangle (Forgive the Past)

Child and Parent

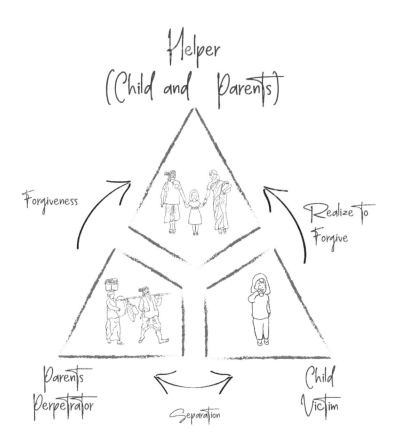

Helper
(Child and Parents)

Forgiveness

Realize to Forgive

Parents Perpetrator

Separation

Child Victim

Chapter Three

I CAN NOW FORGIVE MY MOM

One truth about life is that once one is an adult, one has the right to live their life however they want it, and no one should have their life determined for them as long as they are not doing anything bad. While this could be true, do we understand this as kids to our parents? No, we never did understand. Once our parents are involved, we feel possessive of them, we want to hold them down to ourselves, but we fail to remember that they also have their own life to live. My siblings and I found ourselves in this situation when we were still little. Life wasn't that pleasant for us after our dad dumped our mom and abandoned us to stay with his new wife. My mom would do everything to give us the best she believed we needed. If we were sick, she would do her best to see us get treated. She was paying all the necessary basic bills of the house. We almost became too comfortable with having her around. I particularly saw how other kids spend a lot of time with their mom; my mom was spending time with us too. Then, suddenly, I started noticing some changes in my mom's life. I couldn't understand what was happening, but I began to understand what was happening. First, my mom started looking damn good compared to before. She was now always wearing her makeup whenever she wanted to leave the house. She stopped telling us about her whereabouts whenever she wanted to leave, but I never asked. Then, there were times that she would return later than she used to.

As things continued, it was obvious that something was up already. So, when I was fourteen, mom called us into the living room because she had something she would love to tell us. She told us clearly that she was getting married. It was a tough blow. I don't think I understood what she was saying even though I was close to her and listening. I was a bit lost for a while. I thought through everything that had happened within that period; she had been looking somewhat different from what we had known her to be looking. She was even happier than she had been since my dad left us and went to stay with his new wife. Then she was always dressing cooler than she used to, and my mom, who never stayed out late, was now returning late at night, and it was now regularly. Everything then started adding up; all the changes I had noticed were because of the new man she was seeing. I had seen him drop her off twice before she broke the news to us. I felt like asking her who the man was, but I didn't; I knew it was not my place to ask. I don't know why I felt this way, but the truth is that I felt like my mom betrayed us. I thought she would always be with us, irrespective of what came our way. When my dad got married to another woman, she felt comfortable keeping us, so I kind of felt like she changed. As I was thinking and saying all these, I forgot something. My mom was a full-blown woman. She wasn't just a full-blown woman; she was a beautiful woman, too. I wasn't the only one feeling bad about this at the time; my siblings were also having issues with this. She could see from our expression that we were not in any way supporting the idea, but mom didn't care. She had already made up her mind that she was getting married. After a while, we were able to bring ourselves to accept the marriage, not like we could stop it if we wanted. Now, another difficulty arose. She was getting married to someone, and we were not allowed to stay with her anymore; she wanted to build a new family with her man, and they already agreed that they would need privacy in their marriage. We were allowed to visit from time to time, but not all the time. This got me very pissed. At that moment, the only thing that kept repeating itself in my mind was that our dad abandoned us, and then our mom was going to abandon us. It looked like none of them wanted to have us in their private life. I hated my dad, but I now hated my mom for doing what she did to us. I saw married women separated from their husbands or whose husbands were dead, but they always did all they could to keep the kids and look after them, but my mom's priority was getting married. She showed us that we were not in any way part of her top priorities; that was what I felt at the time.

My siblings and I were mad; we hated the man who would marry her because we felt he was taking our mom away from us. If we could do anything to stop him, we would have done that. I thought of several ways to approach the man my mom was going to get married to; I couldn't bring myself to approach him and talk to him; at least I wasn't as little as I used to be when my dad left us. So, things continued smoothly, and my mom married this man. After the marriage began, I noticed something different about my mom, which I rarely saw when she was with my dad. She looked wonderful, and that was not all that there was to it; my mom was now always looking happy. Getting married again was one of the best things that ever happened to her. The man she married treated her as if she was his life. The fact that my mom was happy meant a lot to me. Though I hated her for leaving us almost on our own and going out to marry a strange man, I felt some sort of relief whenever I saw how happy she was. It took time before I could come to terms fully with the fact that my mom abandoned my other siblings and me. Not like she abandoned us or was no longer playing the role of a mom to us. She did her best, but we just don't like that she got married to someone else.

I realized something about all that my mom did as I grew up. My dad broke my mom's heart, and since they had divorced, she wasn't looking cheerful the way she always was. She smiled, and the big laughter we knew her for became rare in the house. My mom deserved to enjoy her life. People who got kids and raised them also have a life to live. They have desires that should be met; they want to be loved by a man who they can share their love with in return. My mom was a woman that was suddenly deprived of the love which she cherished; I didn't know if she gave up on love before she met the man she remarried to, but when she met this man, she was so much in love with him, that it gave her deep happiness. These were all enough to realize that I wasn't entirely correct when trying to make my mom not get married again. I kind of put myself in her shoes; I imagined what she was going through each time she remembered my dad was with another woman; I realized that she had given us all the love she got, that she needed some love too for herself. I thought how she was brought up, a child of the war, always sheltering and in the constant fear of death. How she started to support her siblings and her family when she was just 17. In my imagination, I met her as a teen, craving for love and attention. By then, I was already in a silent vicious circle. However, I didn't always make it obvious; I later decided it was time to put my acts together, it was time to start living in reality, the reality that my mom got her own life to live, and she was living it to the fullest. I forgave my mom for marrying another man and leaving us out of it; I forgave her. I don't know about my siblings.

My mom was the only mom I got in the entire world; I wasted years mourning over why she had to marry another person. I felt troubled that we weren't allowed to live with her. I thought it was unkind to us because we had been living with her all our lives, and we preferred to stay with her rather than with our dad, while our dad wasn't quite interested in keeping us around at the time. I wasted many years in the vicious circle, but I decided to break out from it by forgiving my mom from the depths of my heart. Now, I have healed completely from it. I can now stay with my mom, laugh, make some jokes, and even play with her, and it was always fun. I am constantly building beautiful memories with her; sometimes, we will hang out with her and my other siblings because they all later grew to get used to the marriage and the arrangement that came with it. Our mom was still with us; the only difference was that we weren't staying in the same house. We called every day, talked every day, and it was a lot of fun. So, after I forgave my mom, I had peace. She had a vacation, too, because she had always had this feeling that I was being somewhat problematic. After all, I wouldn't say I liked the fact that she got married. It was affecting her somehow, but now everyone had been free. Everyone is pleased, and above all, my mom is enjoying her marriage to the end. This is what forgiveness does. It healed me from the hate I accumulated for my mom over the years, and in some ways, it also cured my mom.

When I look at the experience with my mom, I realize that there are so many people out there like me. There are so many people out there who found themselves in the same situation I did back then, and I want to let them know that the feeling of hate and disgust they are feeling is pretty understandable, but I want them to break out from it now. They shouldn't dwell on it for too long. A good child should wish for the happiness of their parents. What matters is the happiness of your mom. If your mom is happy with the man she decided to settle down with, you should be happy for her. Remember, she is the only mom you've got; you will never get another like her. Don't allow prolonged hate and disgust to take away your chances of building beautiful memories with your mom. Don't allow it to stay in you for too long; you will end up regretting it if you allow it to. Break out from the vicious circle; you will be happy you did.

Identity

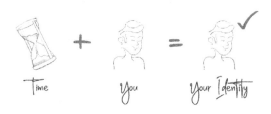

Time + You = Your Identity

Positive Imagination

Actual Sorry Identity

Future Positives

Chapter Four

I CAN NOW FORGIVE MY SISTER

There is this thing about having people who love you. When you have people who love and care for you, there are some decisions that you are not allowed to take without putting them into consideration. Yes, it's your life, and it is yours to live the way you believe is best for you. It is yours to enjoy it the way you like, and it is yours not to enjoy it if you prefer. Still, even though you have the express right to decide how you want to live your life, it is selfish to make some key decisions without considering those that love you, those you call family. Imagine the life of a woman who has cancer as an example; she is married to this man who loves her with all his heart and has two beautiful kids. She loves her husband and kids so dearly; she doesn't want anything to put them in pain. Now, she was diagnosed with cancer, and the cancer wasn't discovered quickly; she needed to act so fast with her treatment. This woman didn't want to go on with the treatment; instead, she decided to hide from her husband that she had cancer, and die slowly. Her reason for not telling her husband was that she didn't want to break his heart. She also didn't want to break the hearts of her kids; she wanted them to be those happy people she had known, so she kept her cancer status away from them. She kept her ailment to herself, and cancer continued to worsen as the days went by. Her husband eventually discovered that she had cancer, and he was crushed. He felt so bad about the whole thing because she didn't tell him. She made a significant decision about her life, but she didn't tell the man she was married to. This was a decision that would go a long way to discern whether she was living or going to die. Still, she took the decision to pass without involving this man she knew that loved her; she didn't consider how he was going to feel after she had died; she didn't even believe how heartbroken her kids were going to feel when they woke up one morning and discover that their mom was dead. Now, it was her decision; it was something she had the right to do for herself, but making this decision and not considering her loved ones amounted to selfishness. After she is dead and gone, they will be the ones to mourn her; they will be the ones to suffer the loss; the dead do not grief, only the living grieve the dead. Cancer is not a death sentence, and this man proved it to his wife. He insisted she go for treatment. After days of little disagreement, his wife decided to go for treatment, and the cancer was treated. She lived many happy years with her husband and kids. What if she had died with the selfish decision she made? What would have been the fate of her husband and kids? How would they have felt that their mom died over something treatable? The thought of it would torment them for a very long time. They will even end up hating their mom, who was really keeping it from them because she loved them and didn't want them to be in pain.

Now, about the issue I had with my sister, who got me pissed. Everybody in the world knows this reality. Covid-19 arrived, ravaging every country in the world. Apart from the fact that it has caused a significant setback to the world's economy, it has brought about a high unemployment rate and has led to an increase in crime. But this is just the little part of it. The central part of it is that Covid-19 led to millions of deaths. Many people died from Covid-19 due to a lack of drugs to treat or control the virus. After extended months of research, they finally found a vaccine. Though this vaccine had been significantly criticized by so many people, considering the speed with which the vaccine became available, the vaccine is all we have at the moment, and has been proven to be somewhat effective. Though the virus kept mutating, we kept finding ways to live past it and get it under control. Despite the discovery of the vaccine, we can't deny the fact that people are dying. People still die from Covid-19, but the truth is that most people dying from the virus are mainly those who refused to get vaccinated. Many have already gotten vaccinated and are dying from the virus, but most of those deaths are people who refused to get the jab. They have their reasons for refusing to get the jab; they keep saying that the vaccine has some side effects considering how quickly it was discovered. Some claim that the vaccine has some potential for causing infertility. There had been different stories, but none had been proven. However, those saying different kinds of stuff about the vaccine still have the right to express their opinion. Yes, we are in a world where everyone has the right to express their view.

So, after saying a lot of bad stuff about the vaccine and how she would never get the shot, my sister got infected by the virus. At first, she thought it was going to go away on its own. Hundreds to thousands of people called the virus that eventually healed without anything. They were never vaccinated, and they hated the idea of being vaccinated. It worked out for them. Other people were like this before the vaccine was discovered. Some of them wished that there was a vaccine at the time, but there was none, so they had to make do with what they got. They boosted their healthy living mechanism, ate the right food, and did other healthy stuff; the virus cleared from their system with time. My sister had always been one of those with a different conspiracy theory about the Covid-19 vaccine. She had another conspiracy theory about the vaccine and had said she would never get vaccinated, no matter what. So, she got infected, and she did all she could do to get the infection out of her system, but the condition was going nowhere. Instead, it continued to worsen. She was isolated. Isolation has been one way we prevent healthy people from getting the virus from sick people. Those who had the virus had to isolate themselves so they didn't end up infecting those who didn't have the virus. This type helps reduce the spread of the virus.

My sister's health kept deteriorating. She insisted that she shouldn't be vaccinated, and at some point, vaccination became the only hope available, but she insisted that she shouldn't be vaccinated. She instructed them not to allow any one of us to come to see her until she was dead. This broke my heart. I was so mad at her. It felt like someone was trying to commit suicide. I know she hated to be vaccinated, I knew she had said a lot of bad stuff about the vaccine, but at that point, it was her last option, but she still refused it, sentencing herself to death without considering any of those who loved her. I felt so bad about it. I hated her for that. I saw it as selfish. I believe she saw it as her way of showing her love; she didn't want us to see her suffering, she didn't want us to witness the pains of watching her die, but it was selfish. It was eating me up from inside, because I was mad at her. She was someone I have known all my life; she was someone that had always been there for me. When my dad left us, she was there; we shared the pain. When my mom found a new partner, we were not happy about it, but she was there; we all shared in it.

We had so many problems as we grew, and she was there during them all, and we all shared in it, and now she was sick and had one shot to life, but she rejected it and even instructed that they keep us out of it. I hated her for it. I hated that she gave up on life without letting us in. I hated the fact that she sentenced herself to death without letting us help. I hated that she told them not to allow us access to her. I hated everything about her. I saw her as a very selfish woman who thought of nobody else but herself, but I had to slow down at some point.

I had to slow down. The best way to live peacefully with people around you who are of different ways of thinking is to bring yourself to the level of their thinking. If you get yourself to the level of their thinking, you will then understand why they did what they did, why they took an action that they took, and why they refused to take specific steps. Yes, I was mad at my sister, but I had to calm myself down and think like her at some point. I had to configure my state of mind to be like hers so I could understand things the way she understood them, especially when she insisted on not taking the vaccine and insisted no family of hers should see her until she was dead.

After imagining her perspective, I concluded that she did all she did out of love for those who loved and cared for her. This is common among some of those who believe they are going to die from a particular ailment. They try to keep their loved ones out of it until the very last moment. I love my sister so much, we love her so much, and she knows this; she didn't want us to feel hurt by watching her die. She knew watching her in that state would be heartbreaking, but we didn't care about that. We wanted to be there for her in her worst moments; that's what family does. There are times when we find ourselves inside real issues, with enormous problems to overcome. Friends might run and stay away; friends avoid identifying with you. Most friends are only there when the going seems palatable. When the going looks right, you see a lot of friends around, but when the going gets tough, you see your friends running away. When real issues surface and friends start giving up or avoiding being with you, the people that step in to save the day are family. The family will always remain by you, no matter how bad things turn around for you. The family will never give up on you, even when everyone gives up on you. Even though my sister gave up on us, we didn't give up on her; we stood by her, albeit we kept a little distance from her due to her being infected by the virus. She later realized that she had made a mistake, but before then, I had already made up my mind to break the vicious circle because I now understood her and why she did what she did.

I know that so many people are disappointed with their family members. These people are mad at their family members for deciding to end their life and never carrying them along into it. If you are angry at a family member for doing this to you, it is very understandable. I was there; I know the feeling. I have heard people say stuff about it; I didn't quite see it as a big deal around then, but I now got to experience it. I now know exactly how it felt to be in that situation where your family member refused to tell you that they were dying. So, if you are there now and mad now, I understand you, I know you, but I want you to know something. Your family member who took that decision took that decision because they love and care for you. They didn't take that decision because they wanted to hurt you.

Some sick people are unable to make significant decisions about their lives by themselves. This is why there is always a family member to sign papers in a hospital before most treatments are commenced. Some family members may just ask the doctor to let them be because they didn't want to be stressed out, even though they know that they might die from whatever made them come to see the doctor in the hospital. This is why a family member, a loved one makes most of the decisions. Now, if you carry hate for a loved one because they refused to let you into the reality of their health status, I understand you. You are correct in feeling that, but I want you to know that you have had enough of being mad at them. It is time to forgive them. It is time to stay beside them. It is time to be their strength. They may think they are going to die from the ailment, but the truth is that most times, they don't die; they end up surviving it. They end up recovering from that particular ailment, and their recovery works out after a family member discovers what they were trying to do and puts a stop to it. Now that you found what your family member is trying to do and it is far from being a reasonable step to take, put an end to it. They have to survive that ailment, and they surely will because you are now part of it. After everything, love is the reason all the while. They couldn't tell you because they love you; you are so mad after discovering that you love them. You all love each other, and that love is strong enough to help them survive. Even if they end up not staying, which can sometimes be the case, make sure that their last moments are memorable. Make sure they leave the world with a smile on their faces. Erase everything that will make you have regrets, forgive them, and heal from your past.

The Drama Triangle (Forgive the Past)

Friend who wronged me

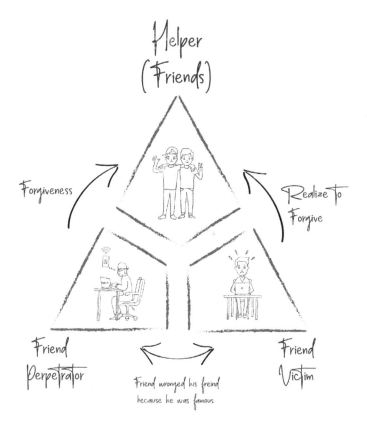

Helper
(Friends)

Forgiveness

Realize To
Forgive

Friend
Perpetrator

Friend
Victim

Friend wronged his freind
because he was famous

Chapter Five

I CAN NOW FORGIVE THE SECOND WIFE OF MY FATHER

No kid is happy when they see their parents having issues with another woman. I know this grown boy who has a dad with a girlfriend. The girlfriend used to be one of his staff, but at some points, one thing led to another, and they started having sex. They became something I don't know if I would call "lovers." The man was married, and he got grown boys who were adults, and this lady knew about all of them. She also knew this man's wife, but she didn't care. I don't think she wants the man to divorce his wife and marry her; it would never come to that because this man loves his family. What mattered was that he was cheating on his kids' mom with this lady. So, when these kids found out about it, they were furious. They confronted this lady several times and even threatened her. She could see how much the kids hated what she was doing with their dad. They didn't want their mom to share their dad with anyone. They didn't want anyone to take what belonged to their mom. I don't know if his mother found out later what was happening, but what I mean is that this man's children did everything they could to stop what their father was doing with this lady without informing their mother.

Before my dad left my mom, he was seeing another woman. It used to cause issues between him and my mom. My mom hated that he was cheating on her, but he was carrying on the affair in a very blunt way. She loved him a lot, so she remained with him even though he cheated on her. One thing was sure; she hated the woman my dad was cheating with. We didn't seem to notice much about what was happening at the time. Moms always love to show their kids that their dad is a great person, even if their dad was falling short of being a great person. This is why some kids keep seeing their dads as their role models without knowing the exact things they've been doing, which were held from them. They only find those things out later, after they've grown. We didn't know what was happening at the time. Our mom wasn't the type who loved showing her kids that she was going through hard times; she always tried to put up a good look for us, which made us not always catch up with the actual situation. Things continued until we started seeing things. We were told that our parents were going to separate. My dad was the one who wanted the divorce; my mom wasn't ready for it. That was when we started paying more attention to things that had been happening, that we hadn't noticed yet. The first day I saw the woman my dad chose over my mom, I was so mad at her. She tried to be nice to me, but I ignored her. I saw her as the woman trying to tear our family apart. Our family wasn't as perfect as it should be because of her. I hated her, and I hated her even more after my dad went through the divorce process. After the divorce, they both moved in and started staying together. I was so mad at my dad, but I couldn't do anything to him because I was still little; he seemed to be enjoying his life with the new woman. For the woman he married, I hated her; I never thought I would ever forgive her for being responsible for tearing our home. I kept telling myself that my mom and dad would have still been married if it wasn't for her. I saw her as the cause of all the problems in our home.

I hated this woman my dad married, but I didn't consider some things. The truth is that if she weren't available for my dad to cheat on my mom with her, my dad would have probably cheated with someone else. He might have even cheated on my mom with several other people. So, it wasn't her fault that my home was torn apart in an absolute sense. My house was already set to be torn apart from how my dad was acting. He was cheating on my mom, so there was no way the marriage between him and my mom would work out because my mom was a self-determined jealous woman. He was cheating on her with this woman, which later resulted in the breakdown of their marriage.

Another thing I came to realize from this woman was that she was a lonely woman. There are things about her I wouldn't like to share, but she was a lonely and empty woman, and that was why she couldn't leave my dad even after she realized that he was married and had kids. I have always thought that she took our father away from us, but that was not the right way to report the story; our father took himself away, he was the one that decided to leave us, and it was never the fault of this woman. She wasn't someone I would like to call a good woman, but she wasn't an evil woman either; she was just someone who wanted to be loved and cared for, wanting nothing from my dad other than his love and the care he had to offer her.

I didn't realize this back then because my mind was clouded in hate. I was in a deep vicious circle. I was in a vicious circle with my dad; I was in a vicious circle with this woman he married and left my mom for. But when the time came, I figured out that I was not a free man at heart; I was punishing myself mentally. The deed was done; my dad was with her, and he was happy. It was a decision he made for himself. He probably didn't love my mom as much as he loved this woman; maybe that was why he cheated on her with this woman, or perhaps he married my mom out of convenience and never loved her. He was pleased with this woman, and she was happy with him too. As much as I hated to admit it, they were a perfect match for each other. Another thing that pushed me to break out of the vicious circle and not allow the hate I had for this woman to control me and take away my joy was that my mom was also happy. The man she ended up with was someone who loved her and treated her better than how my dad treated her when they were married. He made her feel so special and treated her as if she was the only one that mattered to him. She was happy; she found the perfect partner for herself. So, it was a long run of hate, anger and pain, but in the end, the three of them were happy. This made me make up my mind that it was time I let it go. I worked on my heart, I conditioned what I thought about her, I accepted her, and with time, I healed from all that had been troubling me about her.

So many families broke up this way. As a child born into a family, you will never be happy seeing your dad leaving your mom, who had done nothing but love him with all she had.

Some kids try to be cool with it, but most kids are never cool with it. You will get to know what they thought about the whole thing when their dad starts living with the woman; whenever they visit their dad or go to stay with their dad, they always take out their aggression on this new woman in every way possible. They make things difficult for her and never allow themselves to get along with her, no matter how much she tries to be good to them. Only a few kids get along with their dad's wife if their dad dumped their mom to marry her, and most of these few took time before they could accept the woman. So, from my experience, there is no need to hate the woman who took over the position meant for your mom; at least don't hate her for too long. There are things you have to consider. Perhaps your parents' marriage was already very toxic. Toxic marriages are behind most domestic violence and even deaths at different homes. When the marriage becomes very toxic and difficult to handle, isn't it better to separate? Imagine losing your dad or your mom over domestic issues and having the other one spend years in jail; how will you feel? Isn't it better they separate and remain alive and work for their happiness? That woman who came in and took your dad away from your mom might be a helper. Yes, she might be a helper. She might have stopped either of your parents from dying. Your dad could have harmed your mom, your mom could have broken your dad, but this woman came in and put a stop to all that.

The moment you start to see her as a helper, you begin to feel the need to let go of all the grudges that you had already built up against her. All the grievances that had gnawed away at you so much, those grudges that had been denied. You are a moment of happiness. As I said, he who refused to forgive is like a warder. Every warder is like a prisoner. The warder will have to stay alert and watch the prisoner. In order words, the warder is a prisoner to the prisoner. So, when you refuse to forgive, you are a prisoner who had imprisoned someone else. Forgive her. Heal from the pains you have held on to for too long. Look at the better side of what she has done; you will find so many reasons to forgive her.

The Drama Trainagle

Forgive the past

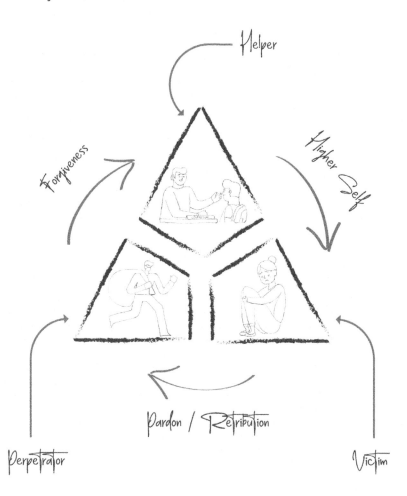

Helper

Higher Self

Forgiveness

Pardon / Retribution

Perpetrator

Victim

Chapter Six

I CAN NOW FULLY FORGIVE MYSELF

Have you ever found yourself in a situation where you sit down and look backward at all the lifestyles you have lived in the past, how you conducted yourself and some of the stuff you do and, after reflection, are ashamed of yourself? Have you ever found yourself in that situation?

Everybody has an eye-opening moment. For some, it comes earlier than for others. For others, it comes later, while for some other people, no matter when that moment comes, they never get to effect any change in their life. I have met a couple of people I used to know way back. I knew some of these people the kind of rough lifestyle they used to live. Now, when I eventually met them, they changed a lot. Some of them even became preachers. Most of them always regret knowing what they know now back then; they believe they would have done better, they think they would have lived a life better than the one they were known to have lived back then.

I knew this man; he was like the second child of his family. I knew him when he was still very much little. I was a bit older than he was. He had this sister that was older than him. I don't think I have ever seen a kid stubborn like this guy. He was never on the same page with his parents. He was a bit luckier than I was when it came to having his dad and mom together. His parents were living together, and they never divorced. They were living happily. Now, this guy was known for one thing, for always being associated with all the bad boys in the neighborhood. In the area, there were always kids every mom and dad told their kids to stay away from. These kids were always known to be a bad influence on any kid associated with them. It was believed that this lousy kid taught kids in the neighborhood how to live a rough lifestyle. They taught kids how to fight, steal, do drugs, and many other kinds of stuff. There was hardly any kid in their league taking their studies seriously.

So, this guy I am talking about was one of these kids. He was involved in many fights; he was doing drugs and even had to drop out of school. His parents were so mad at him when he stopped going to high school. They did all they could to get his ass together, but they couldn't. After some years, his mom died. I think she was ill or something. Then some years later, his dad died. He was left on his own. His sister wasn't living with them, to begin with; she had been living with a relative since she was little. At that moment, he realized that he was literally on his own. He was so stubborn that he didn't make time to spend good moments with his parents. He didn't finish high school, and he had nothing to his name. His parents were average citizens who didn't have much.

His brain almost got it together when his dad became ill. He spent almost everything they had while his dad was sick. Everything was gone. He became humbled with nothing. The last time I saw him, he was filled with regret. He told me he couldn't forgive himself for his lifestyle back then. He told me he wished he could turn back the hands of the clock so that he would have treated his parents better. I used to envy him back then because his parents were living together, but he still wasn't the son they wanted him to be. I'm disgusted when I think back to the promiscuous lifestyle I had in my early first marriage. I had many wounds to heal, inherent injuries to overcome, and many inherent injuries to conquer. I was fighting a series of depressions. While I would not like to excuse my actions, I was drawn to other women. It was challenging to be true to myself at the time. Those moments are what I remember most. My wife was the best woman at this time I could ask for. I couldn't think of a better woman. Although she was all I needed, I was still surrounded by other women. Once I got control of myself, my promiscuous lifestyle became a part of my intrinsic injuries. It was a vicious cycle between myself and it. While I could get out of other vicious circles, another one seemed more pervasive than my control. I hated myself to the end. I felt so bad. I often felt like crying whenever I saw my wife. It was terrible for me. It made me feel filthy and deserving. It took a lot to keep my sanity during those moments. It was clear that I couldn't blame myself for the past. The mistakes I made in my past are gone. I had to stop blaming myself. Instead, I decided to concentrate on the present. I should learn from every mistake I make and make the best of it to help me in the future. I won the battle and ended the vicious cycle between myself and others. I was finally able to forgive myself. My first wife was too young to cope with that. She couldn't, forgive, and her love dried out. We got divorced, and she found another partner. I was free to stop torturing myself and crying about the milk that had been spilled all around. I accepted self-forgiveness and was able to heal.

Some people out there could find their life purpose due to the past life they lived. Some therapists who help counsel drug addicts were once drug addicts. Most marriage therapists had it very rough before they became marriage coaches. No matter the lifestyle you lived when you were in the dark, don't allow it to haunt you for too long. Don't punish yourself over a mistake you made when you were still in the dark. It can only be possible for some people who had been in the night before to tell others how bad it is to be in the dark. See your past lifestyle as a lesson, forgive yourself, and heal.

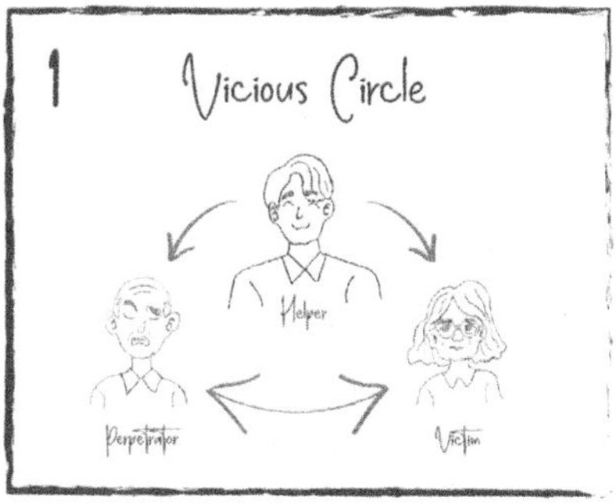
1
Vicious Circle
Helper
Perpetrator
Victim

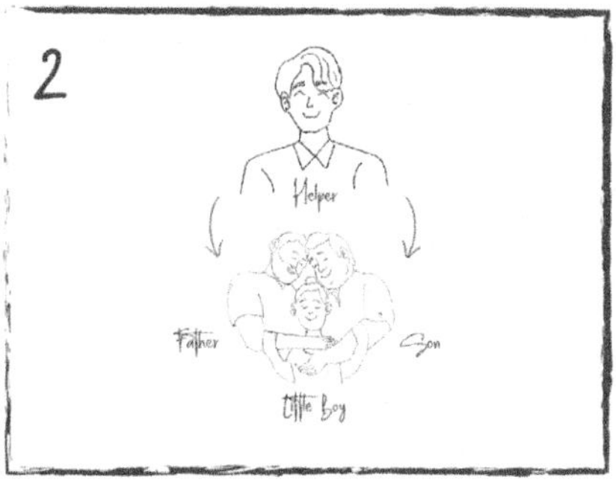
2
Helper
Father
Son
Little Boy

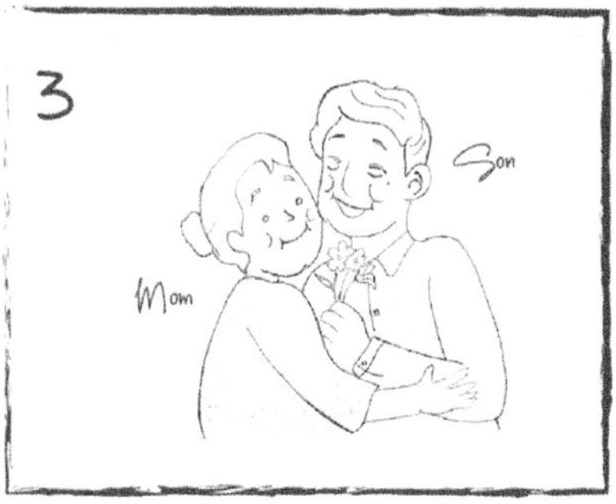
3
Son
Mom

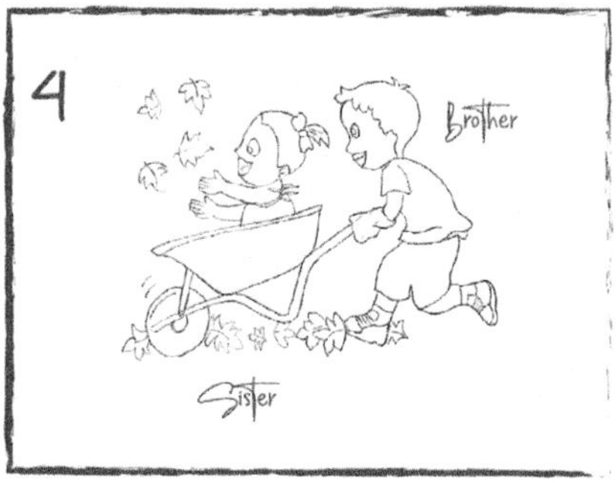
4
Brother
Sister

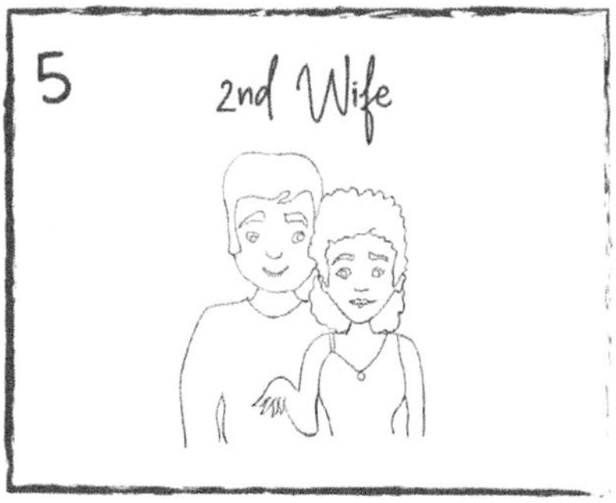
5
2nd Wife

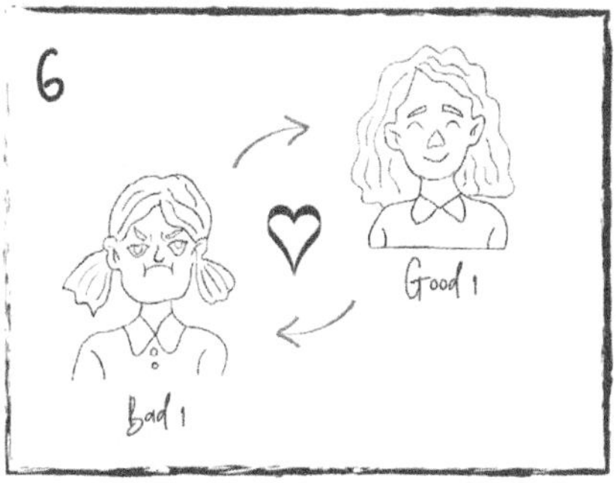
6
Good 1
Bad 1

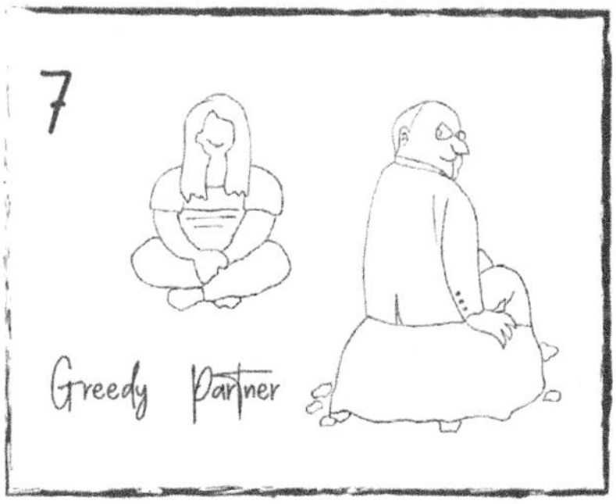
7
Greedy Partner

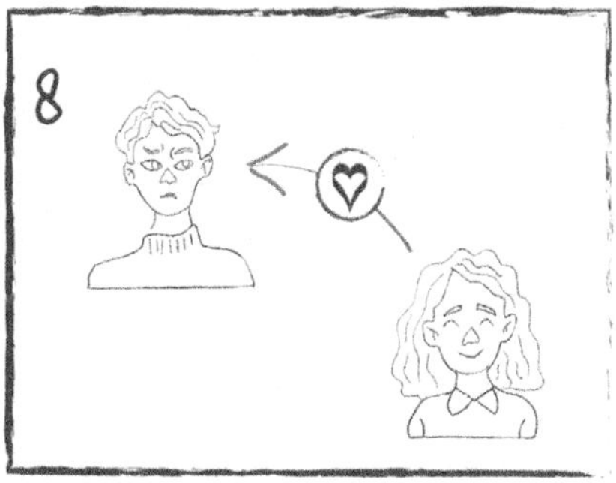
8

Chapter Seven

I CAN NOW FULLY FORGIVE MY Co-Founder

L ife does not always go as planned. Sometimes, you plan the way you want your life to go, you put every mechanism you believe will get your plans to work into motion, you expect everything to move ideally to achieve that very goal which you have in life but, in the end, you failed to achieve that goal you had in mind — even though you did your very best to see to the achievement of that goal. Nothing hits someone so badly like planning your life, and after everything, something comes up and ruins all your plans that you have put together and had fully set your mind to it.

Sometimes, you put together a plan on how you want your life to go. Your project may not be much of a great one, but the most certain thing about your program is that it leads to survival. It might not be something that will make you rich overnight; it might be something that will take a long time to shoot you big, you might need a miracle to make it very big from your plan in a short run, but you know that you will be able to survive from your project. Now, while trying to execute your plan, something comes up; this thing that comes up was so sudden, it came out of nowhere, but it has the potential to turn your life around for good. You didn't plan for this, but you decided to drop your plan and follow this new deal because it looked promising.

This was the situation I found myself in. I had my plans; it might not be seen as the best of projects, but I knew I would do well in it and might make it big with time. Then, this friend came to me with a better deal. He had a plan. He let me into his dream, and his plan almost sounded better than my own. It was something I had never thought about. It was a plan on how to establish an ad agency. He wanted me to join him so that we could do it together. He believed I got what it takes to move the agency forward. I accepted the plan he had because it looked more promising than the plan that I had. We put his plan into Motion immediately. We established the ad agency and started doing what we believed would make the agency known to people who needed our services. We also ensured we did an excellent job for every client who brought work to us.

I have always believed that doing an excellent job was the best way to get more customers; I always prioritized doing a fantastic job above everything when handling a client. So, within a short while, our ad agency started growing so big. We were making reasonably enough money, we were growing popular in the industry, our clients were always happy with the job we did for them, and they always enjoyed referring more clients to us. Things were going so well until after three years. My partner, with whom I always ran the agency, started acting strangely. At first, I couldn't understand what was going on until he told me clearly that he was done sharing the ownership of the ad agency with me; he wanted me out so that he could own it alone. It was a very disappointing experience. He changed my plans and brought me into another project which was his; then, I settled into his plans. Things were now going well, and I was going to make more plans ahead of his dreams that we had already conquered; he then came up to shatter all the sweat I had put to keep the agency running. I was very pissed. He was very selfish. I hated him to the last. I didn't know someone could be that selfish. It was an experience that ruined me for a while. It was my means of livelihood that he tried to take from me. I fell out with him. He became someone I saw as my enemy. He became someone I hated, like the devil himself.

I regretted dropping my plans to follow his. For a long time, I hated him, I despised everything about him, but there was a twist to all these things. Every disappointment has a way to turn into a blessing. If I were still running the agency with him, I wouldn't have made it this big in my space; I wouldn't have thought about having my agency. Then, it felt like I was being kicked out of the game, but it was actually a stepping stone for me to make it big. If it weren't that bad for me then, I wouldn't have had any reason to search for an alternative, an alternative that turned out to be the best option ever. I was mad at him at first, but he was a helper; he helped me by making me feel uncomfortable.

When you become uncomfortable with the current state, you find yourself; only then will you be pushed to make a move. Some people are still at a spot in life because they feel too comfortable with the little they get. I was not getting a lot, the one I had, and I was pleased with it, but then he made me uncomfortable. That was when I had to work; I had to move and exploit my potential. I was mad at him initially, but I decided to forgive him. I decided to let it go because I found a way to become a new person; I no longer lived in hate; I had to break the vicious cycle.

In this life, people you trust will betray you. People you rely on will make you regret ever relying on them; they will disappoint you, but the truth is that they have to disappoint you so you can find an alternative. They have to disappoint you for you to find a better option. They have to disappoint you to feel uncomfortable so you can get something better and more significant. Don't allow the hate they pushed you into suppress you for too long; forgive them and move on.

Let Go Process

My Belief
Neutral
Belief
Belief
Experienced
My Belief

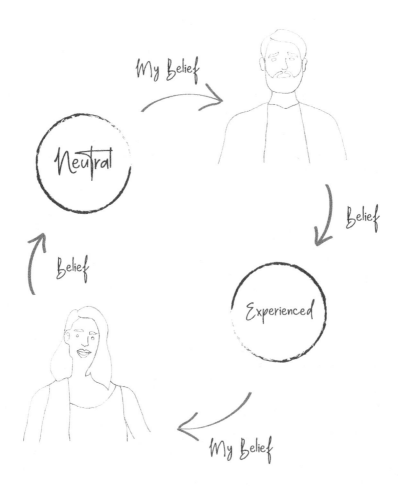

Chapter Eight

I CAN NOW FORGIVE ALL MY EX-PARTNERS

We live in a world where people who are capable of helping people, who are capable of fixing people's lives, ignore them and act as if they don't know that these people need help; they work as if they don't feel concerned. Some of these people refuse to help people even after they see how badly they needed to be supported, acting as a result of a series of bitter experiences they had when they tried to help some people they believed required their help. They tried to help someone they thought was in particular need of their service, but this person they decided to help turned around and stabbed them in their back; he betrayed them and took full advantage of them. As a result, these people now develop a very thick skin that they don't feel any form of sympathy whenever they see people they believe need their help.

There was this man that was driving on a lonely road. He saw someone standing beside the street who seemed to be stranded as he was going. This person asked for a lift. He decided to help this person and carried him in his car, but as they were still on their way, he pulled a gun on him. He stole from him and even shot at him; he was lucky to survive the gunshot. Now, will this person who had this experience ever help anybody stranded on the road again? Never!

In my situation, I had partners who were friends; they met me and begged me to allow them into my publishing business. They wanted to learn and join me in the industry. I have always been the type that loved reaching out to people who I believe need my help. They needed my help, and I was obliged to help them. After they remained with me and learned everything, once they got the chance to betray me, none of them ever looked back; they betrayed me. I was surprised; these were people I helped, these were people whose lives I accepted to fix, but they betrayed me. They stabbed me in the back when I least expected. Some of these people were my best friends. Most of them were spies. They spied on my business; they then went on and opened theirs. They never gave me the full details of what they wanted. If they had told me they had intentions of opening theirs, I wouldn't have felt bad about it, I would have still helped them. My publishing business was to edit cross media (print + online) in each city or touristic destination. It was crazy – everybody wanted to be part of this new story. So a lot of people approached me to be the one who will be the exclusive partner in a specific city. Also, my closest friends asked me - and I ranked them first. I put a lot of very talented and experienced people off. But they played me. I felt betrayed whenever they did this to me. I have gone through a lot in life; at this point, I never want anything that will keep me in a vicious circle. I knew how difficult it was for me to be able to break out from most of the vicious circles I found myself in the past, so I had to do all I could to escape getting into anyone. I had to forgive them, yes, I did forgive them, and from the depth of my heart, I am thrilled when I see them doing well in their businesses, and I do my best to show them that I don't have anything against them, despite how they played a smart one on me. I am at a better level now. My peace of mind, my mental health, mean a lot to me; with my peace of mind and my mental health being intact, I can achieve a lot.

Forgiveness thought the hard way

When I was still a boy in my teens, there was this couple I saw sometimes in my neighborhood; they were a perfect definition of what people call an ideal couple. They rarely had disagreements and were always looking happy. At that point, they were yet to have kids. As a teen, I was still growing into knowing what love was all about. At my age then, I had friends that would tell me some issues they were having with their girlfriends, and I would kind of offer solutions to them. At that time, I was yet to have a girlfriend, but I was like the person everyone always wanted to get his opinion about what wasn't going right in their lives.

From what I have learned about love, I believe that something is not meant to be forgiven. As long as love was concerned, some actions were never forgiven, and one of those I believed at the time was cheating. So, this couple living in my neighborhood never had issues, but I noticed something about this woman's husband; he had this friend who constantly visited him whenever his wife was not at home. This friend was a male, so I never saw it as anything, just that he had other friends, and these friends used to visit sometimes when his wife was around, but this one I was talking about never visited when his wife was around. He wasn't visiting every day, The husband typically leaves to work with his wife every morning, but whenever he leaves for work, he never returns to the house before work is over for the day unless this friend of his was visiting. There were times he returned home with this friend of his, and there were times this friend of his just walked in some minutes after he had returned. I never saw this to be odd, and others in the neighborhood that had noticed a bit of it never saw it to be wrong.

So, one faithful day, I was at home that day I didn't go to school because I was somewhat sick. I was just seated before the house because I was already bored from sitting inside the house. Most of the kids in the neighborhood had already left for school, so I was the only kid in the community. Then, around 10:00 AM – I wasn't with my watch as I was seated before the house, but I knew it was around that time – this man came back home and entered his house. About ten minutes later, his friend came in and entered the house. It was this friend who had never visited when his wife was around. They usually stay in the house for like an hour and thirty minutes or close to two hours before they would both leave the house. But I noticed about forty minutes later, the wife of this man came back home. She was in haste as if something was chasing after her. She opened the door and entered the house. Within a minute, I started hearing screams. I couldn't understand what was happening. I knew the woman was screaming; I didn't know if this man was beating up his wife. I became very interested in what was happening; Within five minutes, this friend of this man, who constantly visited this woman's husband whenever the woman wasn't around, left the house. He wasn't looking happy. The man and his wife remained inside. I returned to the inside of our house, but I stayed close to the window and tried to eavesdrop. This couple remained inside the house for what looked like an hour. The husband later left the house, but the wife didn't leave the house again throughout that day. She remained right inside the house. I didn't hear her scream again, but I also noticed that she didn't go to work the next day because her husband went to work alone.

The day she screamed changed a lot of things in their relationship. I never saw this couple walk again on the street, holding hands and having beautiful conversations. I never saw them doing things that couples out there do. Two weeks after that incident, the wife moved out of the neighborhood. I later learned that she filed for divorce. The husband looked very sad after his wife left. Within months, the man's friend started visiting again. This time around, he visited more often than when this man's wife was still living with him. Soon, the marriage between this man and his wife ended. Later, this man who was visiting him moved into the apartment to stay with him. I was a teen at the time, so I couldn't catch up quickly on what the whole issue was about, but I figured everything out later. This man who got divorced by his wife was a closeted homosexual. I think he wanted to live like most men out there, and he was trying to hide his sexuality around then. His wife had married him thinking that he was a straight man; she never knew he was gay; she only found out the day she discovered them, probably having sex at the time.

Now, I never saw the wife of this man again in the house, not immediately. It took more than a year before I could see her again in the place. When I saw her again, she looked pleased, and she was kind of friends with her ex-husband, whom she divorced after she found out he was gay. There were times she would visit the house when the guy that moved in to stay with her ex-husband was around. My point is that they became friends. She was furious when she was moving out of the house. She felt offended and betrayed, but close to two years later, she returned to her husband differently, though not as his wife, but as his best friend.

This is what I call forgiveness. Forgiveness is when you pardon someone over something you believe was wrong, which they did to you. When you waive any negative feeling or desire for punishment for someone after they had done something against you, that's when you decide to put away all the hate you have for someone, all the grudges you had accumulated for someone as a result of something they did to you in the past that upset you.

Forgiveness is not just based on the relationship you have shared with someone. Forgiveness is not only limited to what others have done to you. Forgiveness can be considered from the angle of what you have done to others. It can be regarded as from what you have done to yourself. Looking from another dimension, forgiveness can also be seen as being able to pardon yourself for what you perceive isn't right, which you have done to others. It is an act of being able to waive from your heart the bitterness that comes with the thought of what you did to others who probably deserve what you did to them or probably didn't deserve what you did to them. From another sense of view, forgiveness is when you can forgive yourself for the wrongs you believe you have done to yourself. It is the state of accepting that you will stop blaming yourself for your actions or inactions that you thought had caused significant damage or sorrow, or unfavorable changes in your life.

Forgiveness entails more of what is perceived rather than what is said. It focuses more on what is felt rather than on what is articulated. It takes more than actions displayed to discern forgiveness; there is more to forgiveness than just an action taken. One can say they forgave you, while in a real sense, they still have real grudges against you in their hearts. One can display an act that shows they forgive you while in their hearts they still felt like punching your face over the incident for which they are claim to have forgiven. It takes more than words articulated to forgive someone. It takes more than actions taken to forgive someone. While words spoken and actions taken could be concrete ways to show forgiveness, the main picture of forgiveness starts with the heart;

You start seeing the other person's vulnerability. You imagine when the now grown-up perpetrator was a little child. How this little child was treated. You discover the wounds and vulnerability on him. Yes – he is also a victim, and if you feel intensely in your heart, you will start feeling compassion. And now you are in a role of a helper and freed yourself from the victim role. Of course, you never can or will forgive the deed – it will remain like it is, but you are able to forgive the perpetrator and free yourself from the chains of the victim's role.

3 Main Forms of Hypnotherapy

Post Hypnotic Suggestions

Self Hypnosis

Hypnoanalytical

My-mindguide.com

Chapter Nine

FORGIVE + HEAL

After my first heartbreak, I was mad at my ex for months. I hated her for what she did to me. I was twenty-two at the time, but I had always seen her at the time as someone I was going to marry. We were so much in love and never thought about a day that would come that the both of us would not even be speaking to each other. I think I gave it my best shot, but it didn't work out. After the breakup, I tried to get back at her in every way I could. I would talk to girls where she could see me make her uncomfortable. I even had to date someone I wasn't quite in love with to make her feel like I had moved on from thinking about her. I wanted to give her that feeling that I wasn't sweating over what she did that eventually led to our break up. There was so much stuff that I did back then that was immature, but the truth of the whole thing was that despite how strong I tried to act, despite how dirty I tried to work, especially when she was watching, I was hurting. I was in pain. I was yet to heal from the pain of what happened that eventually led to our breakup. Everything I was doing after our breakup was mainly to get back at her, but I was in another way ruining myself. I didn't recognize myself in some of the things I was doing. I had to be putting up a different attitude; why? Because I was in pain. I wanted to hurt her, but the natural person I was hurting was myself because I was becoming that moron that I had always hated all my life. All these were happening because I was yet to heal from all the pain I believed she caused me.

Remember, I said that forgiveness is more of what is perceived or felt than articulated and shown in action. The difference between the state of what is perceived and the start of what is spoken and put into action once forgiveness was concerned is "the act of being healed." You can continue saying you have forgiven someone a hundred times every day, but you have genuinely yet to forgive that person. You can continue showing in your actions that you have forgiven someone, day in and day out, but in a real sense, you haven't yet. Everything centers on whether you have truly healed from the pain caused to you by the person you are claiming to have forgiven.

Forgiveness cannot be complete without healing. There is no way you can truly forgive someone if you have not truly healed from the pain you believed they caused you when they did something that broke your heart. Healing goes a long way to make a significant difference between who is acting to have forgiven someone and who has forgiven someone.

Healing has a lot to do when someone is trying to forgive themself over something they believe they had done to themselves or the people around them.

There is no way you can genuinely forgive yourself when you are yet to heal from the emotional torture you keep inflicting

on yourself due to what you believed you did to others or what you thought you did to yourself.

People are living with regrets. They keep blaming themselves for something they believe they should have done differently. They keep blaming themselves because they think if they had done something differently, the result would have probably been different from what it was. They think if they had treated this person differently, he probably wouldn't have suffered all he suffered because of them. They believe that if they had ignored this person, if they had refused to help this person, if they had refused to trust this person, this person wouldn't have treated them the way they had treated them. This person that had treated them so wrongly wouldn't have been close enough to them to be able to treat them the way they treated them. They believe that life would have become better for them if they had done this or that. They think that if they had taken action or avoided taking a particular activity, they wouldn't have found themselves in the state they are currently in. They continue to blame themselves or blame the people who had hurt them. When people find themselves in situations like this, they cannot heal. They still have a long way to walk on the road to forgiveness.

There is this belief that is common among most rape victims. One of the main reasons why most rape victims feel so depressed and even become suicidal is very much connected to the fact that they keep blaming themselves for what had happened to them.

They believe that they have, in a great way, caused the rape that had happened to them. Some will blame themselves for allowing the rapist to be too close to them. The rapist could be a friend. He could be someone they trusted, a friend they never thought would ever take advantage of them, but he did. These girls will blame themselves and wish that if they had done something different with this friend, he wouldn't have raped them. They will blame themselves by saying that if they hadn't accepted him as their friend, if they hadn't trusted him, he wouldn't have raped them. They will be telling themselves if they hadn't gone to his house the day they went to his house, he wouldn't have abused them sexually. They blame themselves by viewing their dressing on the day of the rape as being inappropriate. They will blame themselves for letting him visit their house. There was this married woman that got a little drunk. She was with this office friend of hers, and he raped her without her knowledge. She was so mad at herself. She was suicidal. She kept blaming herself and telling herself that if she hadn't gotten drunk, he wouldn't have raped her. The thought of her being raped because she trusted this friend tormented her, but what tormented her more was the thought of herself being drunk. She felt bad about herself. There are rape victims that will even go so far as to blame themselves for not being able to combat enough to stop the rape. They will blame themselves for not kicking their abuser off them to stop the rape; they will blame themselves for not being able to bite him so hard they would get off them. They will blame themselves for not inflicting enough wounds on him which should have given them an upper hand towards stopping the rape.

Some women got raped at gunpoint. Even though, in reality, their rapist would have shot them if they tried to do anything to stop the rape or if they tried making things difficult for him, they still blame themselves for not doing one thing or the other thing. Some of the things they blame themselves for are pretty impossible because the rapist had a gun, but they still blame themselves. Some other people were raped at gunpoint during a robbery incident. Their husband was probably there when the rape happened. They blame their husbands for not saving them when the rape was going on. They also blame themselves for not being to do something too. The fact that there was a weapon that could have caused the death of someone becomes unreasonable to them. In another way, their husbands are not left out of the blame game. Their husbands will either be blaming them for not stopping the rape. Like the one I mentioned that was raped because she was drunk, her husband accused her a lot for it, and it almost tore down their marriage. Some women were raped at gunpoint during a robbery incident; their husbands also blame themselves. Like the woman who was raped, they wished and regretted that they would have done something differently to stop the rape.

The truth of the matter is that for a rape victim to start making progress towards healing, the first step she has to take is to stop blaming any other person other than the man who had descended to the level of a lower animal to rape her. He is the only one that ought to be blamed for the rape. It is usual for thoughts to come in. It is normal for regrets to go in, but the only person to be blamed for the rape is the rapist. It also is not the person that was there when the rape occurred, the primary and only person to be blamed for everything is the person that carried out the rape. Before you blame your significant other, remember he or she is suffering too. Whether with or without her consent, sex did happen. It must be very traumatic to hear or notice that the woman you love had sex with someone else; it will be traumatic and destabilizing to witness this sex happen right before you and not be able to do anything to stop it. Watching the woman you love being raped by another man must be very traumatic and excruciatingly painful. Once a woman is raped, she suffers a lot; everyone suffers too. Some of those around her will blame themselves for allowing her to be close to the man who eventually raped her. Some will be blaming themselves for introducing her to the man that raped her; some other people will be blaming themselves for not being able to stop the rape. And, most times, after a woman goes through rape, the rape itself gives birth to a woman different from the woman that everyone around her used to know. It is one of the biggest punches that everyone around the rape victim may live with. Some rape victims don't recover fully from the trauma caused by the rape they went through.

So, there is blame going on left and right. The blame militates forgiveness from coming in. You might be right that you should have done this or that, but that isn't an excuse for being raped. It is not an excuse to justify the action of the rapist. Whatever blame you have to throw at yourself or someone or some people around you, they are baseless. As I already said, the person you should blame is the rapist. That is the only way to start healing. You have to forgive yourself for whatever role you think you have played. In a real sense, you did nothing; it is a dangerous act to continue blaming yourself. It is a detrimental act on yourself to continue blaming some people around you.

When you continue to blame some people around you, you will have a big problem with healing. Healing can never come in unless you have done what's needed.

One thing that needs to be done before healing will come by forgiving yourself of whatever role you think you played. No one wants to harm themselves. No one wants to do things that will put them in harm's way. No one wants to inflict injury on themselves. Everyone wants the very best for themselves; this is why you have to accept that there is nothing you should have done differently. You have to forgive yourself. Your healing starts coming towards you the moment you learn to forgive yourself. Your life will remain stagnant if you continue to play this blame game. You will stay at a spot while others continue to run. You will remain seated while others are standing; you have to get up and start walking or even running; first, you have to forgive yourself, then you can heal.

Healing from war traumata?

Most young men who resigned from the army after being sent on a special mission always come back home differently from how they were before they left for the particular task. Before these people left, they were so lively; they were pleased people who liked to have fun; they did everything they could to be comfortable and even made people around them happy. Many people wanted to have the great life they believed they had and even did their best to keep them as friends. So, this army officer goes to war and then returns a different person from what those around him used to know him as. After a war operation, many army officers come back home injured. Some come back home with amputated legs. Some come back home with amputated hands; some come back home with different injuries on their bodies. When they come back home, they get proper medical treatment for their injuries. There are some who go to the war front and return with no physical injuries. Still, these people are profoundly injured than people around them will notice immediately. They are massive injuries, just that their injuries are different from the physical injuries that were common among other people. These injuries will not be noticed immediately, but they kind of find their way out with time. They find their ways out because they can't be hidden for too long. The victim might be doing their best to suppress it and look cool before everyone, but after a while, everything settles, and people around them start seeing how damaged they became. These army veterans saw a lot on the battlefield. They saw people torn apart by war weapons. They saw humans die as if they were worth nothing. They saw their comrades die in the blink of an eye. Some of them, their comrades, were killed in their hands. They saw people they had trained with for long, people they shared locker rooms with, people they came to accept as their brothers and their sisters die in one of the cruelest ways, and they couldn't do anything to save them. Some of these people died because they were trying to protect them. Some of them saw a grenade coming and had to stand in the way to preserve this injured person from being killed by the grenade and die to protect their comrade. This can tear these veterans apart. All they have seen and experienced continue haunting them in the form of nightmares. They could hear the voices of their comrades when they were in their last moments; they could listen to the last words of their comrades repeating themselves in their heads. This hit them so badly.

The fact that someone they loved died to protect them is a reality that haunts them for a very long time. They knew this person that died had loved ones. This person who died may have had a wife and kids, or an old mom waiting for him to return. And when this person that got to survive because of the sacrifice their comrade made returns to see all that their comrade left behind, it tears them apart and haunts them. They start seeing themselves as weaklings. They start believing that they were cowards, which is why they didn't die the way others close to them died on the battlefield. They began to see themselves as big-time betrayers because they managed to survive the battlefield while others that were close to them who shared the battlefield with them died on the battlefield. At first, they will be acting cool; they will be faking smiles but with time, real sadness sets in.

The regret becomes too big for them to handle. They start blaming themselves. They start wishing they had done things differently to have saved some of their comrades that didn't make it out of the battlefield. Some of them begin replaying some of the battlefield scenes; they start visualizing how things happened and start seeing how they should have done things differently to save the day. Real frustration sets in when this continues for a long time, and then depression comes in. A significant sum of them become suicidal, and out of those that become suicidal, some of them pull the trigger on themselves. They give up on life because they have already concluded in their hearts that they don't deserve to be living. This is the reality of many army veterans who resigned from the army after tasting the battlefield.

Being a survivor from the battlefield shows you are lucky. It is a gift. It doesn't mean you are more intelligent than others who died on the battlefield. This is because once on the battlefield, you could get shot at from anywhere. Sometimes, tactical understanding doesn't go as planned.

Most importantly, it doesn't mean that you are an imposter. That you didn't die like others doesn't in any way make you unworthy of living. It doesn't make you less of a real soldier. Before the war, you were afraid. Before you got into the battlefield, you feared death. You knew you might never return home to meet your loved ones. You knew you would most likely not get to be with all of those you have spent quality time with before going into the battle; yes, you knew that some of your comrades would die on the battlefield. You were afraid. Despite your fear, you could take your weapon and go into the battlefield. That is courage. Your courage which was built from the strong desire to protect the sovereignty of your country drove you into suppressing your fears and taking the battlefield to face your enemy. You could have changed your mind and maybe deserted, but you didn't. Your enemy was dreadful; they were ruthless, they made you remember the fears in your heart before you got into the battlefield, but you still managed to remain standing and fighting back as hard as you could. If you were a coward, you wouldn't have remained standing. If you were a coward, as you are thinking, there are things you would have done to protect your skin, but you didn't. You stood at the waterfront, and you remained on the battlefield until you got an order that it was over. You followed orders till the very last. Cowards would have disobeyed orders to save their skin, but you didn't. Do you now see that you are not a coward? Do you now know that you did more than your best? That comrade of yours that died on the battlefield was never your fault that they died. There was nothing you really could have done to save them. Even if you had the opportunity to protect them and you didn't, it doesn't in any way make you a coward. Life is all about survival. You could have died saving them. Imagine what would have happened if you had been killed. Imagine your family, your loved ones, the pains they would have endured if you had died on the battlefield, so there is no need to continue killing yourself with regret. There is no need to continue blaming yourself over something you never really had control over. You have to forgive yourself. You have to heal from all the pains you have accumulated in your heart, and the only way through which you can recover is by forgiving yourself.

When two people of different ideologies from different environments meet together, there are bound to be times when there will be some sort of misunderstanding. In having a misunderstanding, someone may end up feeling used or cheated. Did your friend – whom you trusted and decided to offer a helping hand to when everyone around them turned their back at them — take advantage of the help you rendered to them? Perhaps all you cared about was how to make things better for them. You put everything on the line to fix their lives. People did come to you to tell you stuff that would dissuade you from helping this friend, but you stood your ground, but in the end, this friend betrayed you. Whenever you remember what they did to you, you become so pissed; you regret helping them, hate them, and believe you will never forgive them for what they did to you. Though you were wronged, maybe you wronged them too, but you never knew. You might be seeing yourself as the victim just as they might be seeing themselves as the victim. You have to forgive them. You have worn never to help others due to the experience you had with this friend; you blame yourself so much for helping them, you have to forgive yourself.

Hate will only give you a myopic view. Yes, I myself, in my stormy days, fell in the trap of hate and repulsion. In this vicious cycle, nobody wins and everybody will lose. After my business partner cheated on me, I sued him and took him to court. What for? A longtime relationship and great memories had been destroyed, lost forever. He wanted to retribute and was then my fiercest competitor. The outcome for both of us was disturbing... Those you are refusing to help today might be those meant to help you tomorrow. Forgive yourself and forgive those that wronged you for you to heal from your pains. You have held onto that pain for too long; it is time to recover from it.

Some people have missed the chance to be in a relationship with their soul mate due to the defensive parameters they had set around them. These people were in this previous relationship which they cherished with all their heart. They did all they could to make the relationship move forward and succeed. They did all they could to make the relationship work. They gave their total commitment, they gave their time, they compromised in every way possible to make the relationship work, but their partner, whom they did all these for, took advantage of their love and broke their heart. After the heartbreak, they were so hurt due to the pains they went through that they decided they wouldn't give their all again in any new relationship. They tell themselves that they had given their all in their previous relationship, and their ex had taken advantage of the love they gave. As a result, these people now build up some sort of defensive parameters.

They do this to protect themselves from the same issue they had before or prevent themselves from doing too much so that they wouldn't have much to lose should the new relationship crumble.

They develop an unpleasant attitude which they use to protect themselves. If this person is a lady, she may see herself as too intelligent for any man that wants to be in a relationship with her. She becomes somewhat selfish but wasn't like this in her previous relationship. Perhaps this new guy is meant to be her soul mate, but due to the ill-treatment he continues to receive from her, he sees her as selfish and can't continue. He breaks up with her. This lady ends up losing a good man, a good man that was meant to be her soul mate. People who put up some sort of smartness to protect themselves due to the previous bitter experience they had in their last relationship end up treating the next person coming into their life badly. This person will not last with them. Her excessive bright attitude will ruin her chances of getting a man far better than her ex. These people that put out this defensive parameter are suffering from their inability to forgive their ex. They are yet to heal completely from the ill-treatment they received from them. Because they have not healed, they will continue to feel bitter and try to put out selfish defense mechanisms to protect themselves. People like this are so upset when an issue concerning them comes up. If you are experiencing this, you are yet to heal from the pains inflicted on you by your ex. You can only be healed if you accept to forgive them.

There is the thing that some people don't know; you can forgive an ex that did wrong stuff against you and still not go back to being in a relationship with them. Forgiving an ex for the ill the ex did to you in the past does not necessarily mean that you will get back in your relationship with them. You may end up going back to them after forgiving them, but it is not a compulsory thing. It is your choice. If you can't forgive your ex, you will have to live a very long time with bitterness. Your bitterness will keep coming into your activities and try to ruin them for you. Forgive your ex, and heal from this bitterness. There is a lot to lose if nothing is done about your hate. Forgive and heal.

Some people are so mad at their parents. Some people are so mad at their parents over something they did to them in the past. They have a lot of hate for their parents. Some people are mad at their parents for controversial reasons, such as not being rich. Yes, some people are mad at their parents because their parents gave birth to them in what they describe as a low-income family. They hate their parents for almost every misfortune that comes their way. If they fail an exam, they may say it is their parents' fault because their parents were asking them to do a few chores at home, thereby taking some of the time they should have used to study. People who act this way always have something they believe their parents had done to them, which they can't forgive. That thing they think their parents had done to them kind of makes them find fault in whatever their parents do. They complain a lot about their parents even when some of the stuff done by their parents are actually what was expected of them. Whatever your parents did to you that makes you feel hate for them, you have to forgive. You can't continue to hate on your parents forever. You will not have them there all the days of your life; being mad at them at times you are meant to be building beautiful memories with them will surely come back to haunt you. You have to forgive them; you have to heal from the pains you believe they have caused you. The only way to do this is to forgive them. Remember that though they are your parents, they are still humans and can never be entirely right even when they claim to be correct.

There are people out there blaming themselves for something they believe they should have done differently. The fact that they did it the way they chose to do it might haunt them a lot. I have seen people in so much pain due to not allowing their parents to spend wonderful last moments with them before they died. I know this man who felt like crying whenever he remembered his experience with his now-dead mom. When she was sick, she was always calling his line to talk to him. He wasn't her only child, but she had always felt comfortable talking to him. So, she kept calling his line one faithful day, and he ignored her call because there was something that was not indispensable, which he was doing at the time. He just missed her call because she was constantly calling. He was told that his mom had died from her ailment the next day. He was so mad at himself. He regretted not responding to her phone calls. He keeps blaming himself and wishes he had done something differently. He keeps being angry at himself and can't stop wishing he listened to what she had to say; he knew she wanted to say something to him. He blames himself a lot. There is this other woman that had been so depressed. In the beginning, she had been depressed due to her husband's death. She missed him so much, his sudden absence in her life affected her so severely, but her depression switched to something else with time. After she spent a long time mourning the death of her husband, she was starting to feel a bit relieved from the pain that came with the loss. But the pain was not going away, so her depression went to another level. She was depressed about something else. Her husband was a military officer. A day before he left for the mission that got him killed, she had a heated argument over some issues they had. She was pissed at him and refused to talk to him throughout the night. He made a few attempts to mend the broken bridge between them, but this woman made things difficult; she wasn't going to have any of it. So, the following day, he got up, kissed her forehead, and left without even saying goodbye. That was the last time she saw him. When he got to the location of his mission, he texted her. The text was the last thing she got from him. The text remained on her phone; she couldn't bring herself to delete it off her phone even after she had deleted countless messages from her phone. She keeps tormenting herself. She keeps wishing the hands of time could be turned backward so she could do things differently. At some points, she would even blame herself for his death because she believed he remained distracted on the battlefield due to being worried over the issue they had and eventually got killed in the process. She knew how troubled he always was whenever they had problems, he was always the one that apologized when he was wrong and even when she was wrong because he couldn't stand having issues in their marriage, but he died. This woman is so guilty that she sometimes becomes suicidal. She feels so guilty for his death. She feels depressed that she couldn't spend the last moment she had the opportunity to spend with him in peace and harmony. This continues to haunt her. This other guy whose mom needed urgent surgery to survive an ailment; he couldn't afford the money required for the surgery. He did all he could, but he couldn't raise enough money for his mom's treatment. She didn't get the surgery, and she died before he could get half of the funds needed for his mom's treatment. This guy can't stop blaming himself. He hates himself for being broke and not affording his mom's treatment. There are so many stories out there about people blaming themselves for one thing or another. They are so bothered that they are depressed about it.

People keep blaming themselves for different reasons. It becomes a big problem when you blame yourself for the death of someone. The question is, does being depressed over an experience as a result of your actions or inactions bring back the lost opportunity? No, it doesn't. If a loved one died and you felt you should have done something different with them. Putting yourself into endless misery because you didn't perform some obligations to or with them before they died will not make you have that lost opportunity again. You have to move on. You have to forgive yourself. You have to heal. Healing will only come when you forgive yourself.

Healing The Past

1 Affect
Desired Feeling
(Place of Relaxation)

Regression

4

5 Hypermnesie
You memorize like
never before

2 Characteristics:
· Pressure
· Heaviness
· Eptyness
· Tight Feeling
· Tight Knot

3 Localisation
· Neck
· Chest
· Stomach

Progression

Chapter Ten

THE VICIOUS RELATION OF PERPETRATOR-VICTIM

If you feel guilty or you think of a person who harmed you, you are in the vicious relation of the perpetrator-victim dynamic.

The victim is that person that believes that they had been wronged. Victims are those that think that they were taken advantage of. They are the people that are not happy because of what had been done to them. These people are generally filled with regret. They wish they had done things differently. They wish they never met the person that turned them into their victim. They can't help but hate this person more and more for what this person had done to them. These people are the victims. Usually, the victims only see things from their side of view. They always think that they were right in everything they did with the person who victimized them. In the victim's eyes, the victim is free from any form of wrongdoings as long as what transpired between them and the perpetrator was concerned.

The perpetrator is that person the victim blames for every woe that has befallen them. The perpetrator is that person the victim believes is the cause of their misfortune. The victim sees the perpetrator as an ingrate, lacking every form of dignity. The victim believes he trusted the perpetrator, he had good intentions towards the perpetrator, but the perpetrator took advantage of everything and released mayhem into their life.

The truth is that, while the victim might be seeing the perpetrator as even and inhuman, the perpetrator, in most cases, has their own story to tell, which the perpetrator believes justified the actions they took against the victim. Have you ever listened to a report from someone about how he was mistreated by someone else and ended up supporting, but later, you had the opportunity to hear the story of the perpetrator, and you finally decided that the person that was seeing himself as the victim was the actual perpetrator. In contrast, the other person was the victim? I have listened to so many stories from people about how badly they were treated by someone I know, but when I got to listen to the other side of the story, I realized that the acclaimed victim role wasn't that clear. Very often, there is a blame game, and if you ever had been at a court and heard all the witnesses which leave you behind confused. There will always be clashes in understanding between people, and when there are clashes in agreement, we start having some people who claim to be perpetrators being victims.

Are you in a vicious perpetrator-victim relationship? You feel pained by what you believe the perpetrator has done to you. What about the one you have done to the perpetrator? What about the one you have done to others around you? How long will you continue to live in the vicious relationship of the perpetrator-victim? People who live in hate hardly make it big in life because they only attack people who live in hate. They say birds of the same feathers fly together. People who live in hate will most likely fly with people who live in hate. This will slow whatever achievement they had stipulated for themselves. There is no way they will live in an aura driven by positivity.

Even if you are mad at the perpetrator, shouldn't there be a limit to how long you should be angry at the perpetrator? Mr./Mrs./Miss Perpetrator, shouldn't there be a limit to how long you will continue hating the victim? At some point, you should give up on your pride; you should come down from your mountain of hate and try to break your vicious relationship between you and the person you see as your perpetrator.

To be able to fix this vicious relationship between the acclaimed victim and the accused perpetrator, there are two questions we will take our time to look into:

The first question to look into is, who is responsible? This question goes deeper than is seen. "Who is responsible" is the most general peculiarity that exists in the most vicious relation of victim-perpetrator. Most people are still insistent on maintaining this relationship due to this question, who is responsible? What does it mean to be responsible? Being responsible is gradually becoming too difficult for people to adopt. Being responsible entails accepting blame for something you believed had gone wrong under your watch; when you own up to your mistakes, you accept that you have done something and request understanding and forgiveness for something wrong you have done. We live in a world where taking responsibility for something is now perceived as a death sentence. People lie a lot. Even in government, when a politician does something that attracts a lot of criticism, this politician looks for ways to dodge taking responsibility for what had been done. Even in businesses, many bosses don't like taking responsibility at work. What they do at first is deny the whole thing. Once it becomes difficult to deny, they look for someone to blame.

In most cases, most of those that end up carrying the blame accepted to carry out the dirty work, which attracted criticism after they got orders to do so by their superior. The superior dodges it and then shifts it to a subordinate. Who is responsible? This is the question we are looking at. The person asking "who is responsible" is not looking for how to break the vicious relationship. This person is in no way looking for how to mend broken bridges. This person still wants to continue wallowing in the cruel relationship even though this person knows it is long overdue to do something about it.

The second question we will be looking at is "what is responsible?" This is the second question we will be looking at from the angle of vicious relation of victim-perpetrator. When you look at this question we are talking about now, you will notice that this question is not interested in the victim's identity. This question is also not interested in knowing who the perpetrator is. Despite how long the vicious relationship has lasted, despite the continued blame games that had erupted between the victim and the perpetrator, the question is just not interested in knowing who the victim is and who the perpetrator is. **The question sees every party as a victim and as a perpetrator.** The question is not interested in criticizing anyone; the question is also not interested in getting anyone punished for any form of misconduct.

Looking at the two questions I have brought up, which we have taken a brief time to analyze, we can see how these two questions affect the vicious relationship between victim-perpetrator. Whoever is asking who is responsible for every issue that comes up is not interested in making peace. This person is so good at finding faults. What this person needs is someone to blame. This person might be wrong in something they had done, but because they want to maintain the position of a victim, they try to look for whom to blame, even if it's their fault. This person has no interest in peace and will increase the already heated vicinity. Anybody asking about what is responsible is interested in one thing, and that is "solution." This person knows that something is wrong. This person knows that it is not right to continue maintaining the vicious relationship of victim and perpetrator.

Some people maintain hostile relations of who is the victim and who is the perpetrator because of the lack of maturity. Perhaps, when they started such association, they lacked enough maturity to handle the situation. Still, now that they had gotten more experience in life and had even gotten a great sense of maturity, they are currently focused on "what is responsible." Some of these people in this vicious relationship had been in it for a long time and had even forgotten the real cause of the cruel association. These people now decide that it is time to fix this problem; they determine that it is time to break the vicious relationship they have with someone they see as a perpetrator or someone who sees them as a perpetrator. They start asking the question, "what is responsible?" Perhaps they are the victim, but they believe they have gone past the stage of identifying as the victim. They are ready to negotiate. They are prepared to make some degree of difference. People like this end up succeeding in breaking the vicious relationship between the victim and the perpetrator.

Have you ever asked yourself why there are no permanent enemies in politics? Politics might be seen as a dangerous venture, but it is a venture that is one of the most prestigious in the world. Politics is very dangerous because it can put out a lot of challenges and depression on those who intend to venture into it. When you are a politician, some people will not be cool with some of the policies you make; these people will be so passionate about how much they hate some or even one of your policies that they will want to do anything to get back to you. We saw in the news what happened to the French President in 2021. 2021 had been a tough year. 2020 was tough, and 2021 was tough, too. The whole world was battling to salvage their economy because Covid-19 caused a lot of damage to the world economy. As a result of the Covid-19 pandemic, the world was thrown into panic. The world was thrown into chaos. There was a lockdown; people had to lock themselves up to protect themselves from getting infected from Covid-19. There was a lot of threat to hunger because the world was locked down, and people couldn't go about their everyday life activities; most people remained in their houses.

Some had to ration their food to be able to survive the lockdown. After the lockdown, the world started getting hit more by the lockdown and the panic the pandemic was causing. Most countries stopped getting money through exports, and even those that exported little were giving them away for almost nothing. Weaker countries couldn't continue to sustain themselves without borrowing from stronger countries. Then, there was this big issue of mass retrenchment of workers from their places of work. Most businesses were finding it difficult to survive. Many companies went bankrupt and closed down; those who were yet to close down started working on how to sustain the existence of their business. Their turnover went low, the money they were getting was significantly reduced because people were not buying as they used to. These companies now started sacking people. A lot of people became unemployed. So many people were frustrated for one reason or another. So, when Macron, the French President, made his way to a public function, he was beaten up by one of those standing and listening to him. The man was so pissed that he forgot the status of the President and assaulted Mr. Macron. It is not easy to rule over a nation. One big issue about being a politician is that your life becomes in the public domain once you venture into politics. If there is anything you did in the past that would look degrading, your political opponents will dig on it and feed it to the media. Politics is a game of numbers; your opponents know this, so they will dig into your past and try to use it to make the people hate you.

While some politicians criticize their opponents constructively, some others criticize their opponents subjectively. They charge them with hate, which makes these politicians not see eye to eye. During election debates, you know how the environment is heated up; some of these politicians look like they are going to fight, at that point, they hate themselves. They want to punch at each other and discredit each other, but in the end, they all know one thing: they are doing all they are doing for their country. In the end, "what is responsible" becomes the banner binding all of them.

You can't maintain a vicious relationship where you are the victim, and another is the perpetrator. You can't. You shouldn't, and you mustn't continue. We will look at the bigger picture in the next chapter.

The Drama Triangle (Forgive the Past)

Harassment

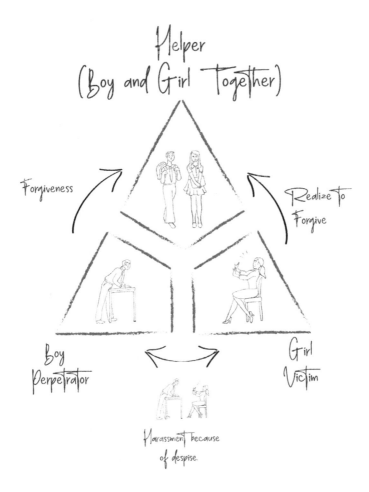

Helper
(Boy and Girl Together)

Forgiveness

Realize to Forgive

Boy
Perpetrator

Girl
Victim

Harassment because
of despise.

Chapter Eleven

THE TRIANGLE PERPETRATOR - VICTIM - HELPER

I already talked about the perpetrator and the victim; let's take a brief look at the helper and then link everything to a triangle.

The helper is that person who assists. The helper is that person who tries to get one out of whatever that troubles that person. The helper could have their gain in mind when trying to help the person who needs to be enabled, but in most cases, the motive to help is high compared to the portion of the gains that the helper had to gain from rendering the help. Some helpers don't care about you; they have a high percentage of their gain. Though they are trying to help you, the main thing that they care about is how to gain a lot from the help they are rendering to you. These people may try to draft a strong agreement before they can help you; this is to make sure they don't end up losing after helping you.

Nevertheless, some helpers just help you because they want to make things better for you. They are not interested in what they stand to gain; the only thing that matters to them is improving their living standard. There is one thing common in every kind of help rendered to someone; the common thing is that the life of the person receiving the service becomes better than it used to be in the past.

Forgiveness centers on breaking the vicious relationship between a perpetrator and a victim. Some people keep asking themselves, why should I forgive this person after all they have done to me? Some people complain that they did everything they could to make life better for this person, they made a lot of sacrifices to make life better for this person, but this person later turned against them. This person took advantage of them. While you are focusing on how much pain this person has caused you, have you considered how this person helped you through the pain this person had caused you? Do you know that you benefited in some ways from the pests this person you are seeing as a perpetrator has caused to you? That victim whom you see as exploitive, do you know he was trying to help you in his way before you decided to take advantage of him? There is a very logical way to view this.

Think of a triangle: perpetrator - the victim - helper. You might be seeing yourself as the victim; they might be seeing themselves as the victim. You might be the perpetrator, or they may be the perpetrator, but I want you to know this. With your positive resources, you can all neutralize, and everybody will have the role of the helper. Being a helper already started among the both of you a long time ago before you had issues;

it even continued even after you had problems, and even now that you are still having issues, you are both still playing the role of a helper.

Let's start with the perpetrator. As the perpetrator, the victim allowed you to do something for you to make things better for you. You were able to become the perpetrator because the victim allowed you to. Now, the question is this: how did the victim enable you to become the perpetrator? The victim allowed you to become the perpetrator by trusting you. If the victim didn't have some element of trust in you, you wouldn't have been able to turn them into a victim. There was a relationship between you and the victim. If it was love, you felt loved. The victim helped you feel loved. That is a help. So many people want to feel loved who never had the opportunity to get love. The victim must have rendered some assistance to you while the relationship lasted; it helped. You must have learned something positive from the victim; that also helps. If it was business, the victim trusted you enough to do business with you, thereby assisting you in making more money; that's helpful. If you are a relative, the victim loved you; the victim cared for you, the victim trusted you, the victim made you feel special and wanted. This is something so many people out there can't get. It is helpful. Then, after there was a breakdown between the both of you, you were mad, you might have been depending on the victim, but you now fought on your own, you struggled to get on your feet, you established yourself, and today you are successful or doing better independently. If you didn't have the issue with the victim, you might still be dependent on the victim. Do you now see the help that came from the breakdown the both of you had? It had been helping from the beginning. It has always helped, and it is still helpful even now that you are reading this.

Then, for the victim, we can't say any less of how the perpetrator helped mold the victim's future. Some victims are thinking about how the perpetrator stole from them; they are talking about how this perpetrator has taken advantage of their kindness. As a victim, do you know that you have gained a lot from this particular perpetrator with whom you are in a vicious relationship? Do you know that this victim was your helper, is your helper, and is still your helper even though you have long cut off your relationship with this perpetrator? I will show you what I mean here: when you were with this perpetrator, what were you gaining from being with this perpetrator? There must have been something. You gained from it; it made you happy and made you come for more; this is helpful. You gained companionship from them. If you had them back those days because of an agreement you had with them related to the business, you made gains from that agreement; they contributed a great chunk of their money to get you rich. This is another form of help from the perpetrator to the victim, which the victim might not be seeing. At the cause of the disagreement, which caused an issue between the perpetrator and the victim, the victim who had grown so much attached to the perpetrator now learned how to be on their own. You have stayed too long with the perpetrator that you have almost forgotten how to do common things on your own; the perpetrator helps you manage most of your businesses. The perpetrator, though he is working on getting things better for themself, becomes your source of dependence. Now, imagine what would have happened if the both of you hadn't gotten to have the issue that tore you apart; you might not have learned how to do things on your own, you might have issues of being dependent on yourself. Today, you are doing so well in your venture; you were able to remain independent because of how you and your perpetrator had been staying in a vicious relationship; this is helpful. Your perpetrator helped you gain independence. Another important way that the perpetrator with whom you have a vicious relationship helps you is that they were very instrumental in bringing out the best in you. When the agreement/friendship between the both of you went sour, your perpetrator forced you to go back to doing what you are doing in a better way. You were in a negative relationship with this perpetrator; there was some sort of competition between the both of you. Both of you wanted to become better than each other, or better still, you wanted to become far better than they will ever be; you started working ten times harder than you did in the past. You gave more of your time to what you were doing; you wanted to show the perpetrator that you could do better than they could ever do, and you worked hard, and you ended up proving yourself. That is another form of help. This perpetrator brought out the best in you. This popular saying says, "the best way to get back to an ex that thought you would never make it big is by being far better than this ex." You never believed that you could do better, but as a result of the quest to do better than your ex whom you saw as a perpetrator, and you have been in a vicious relationship with them, you became better. In the competition, you drew in your heart with them; you ended up winning the competition with the very help of this perpetrator whom you wanted to prove wrong for what they did to you in the past. So, the perpetrator helped you, even with the pains you believed they caused you.

The pains brought out the best in me; the pains became my stepping stone to doing more and getting more. The pain of being abondand at 16 helped me to be streetwise. To gain self-confidence and to adapt quickly to changing situations. I'm resilient now, and even Covid 19 doesn't bother me at all. If you learned nothing from all the time you spent with the perpetrator with whom you are currently in a vicious relationship, you must not have been monitoring yourself properly. From the experience you had with this perpetrator, what did you learn? You learned to watch whom you are trusting. You believe you trusted this perpetrator, and the perpetrator took advantage of it. From your experience, you already figured out that if you go out to trust someone again that easily, you might get worse treatment than the one you got from this perpetrator with whom you are in a vicious relationship. Trust is not meant to be given; trust is earned. You get to trust someone after different functions the person had performed before you or at your back which you get to see or perceive. You don't make yourself trust someone; someone makes you trust them. It means that someone has to work to get your trust, and you are not the one to work your way into trusting someone. But some people reduce the standards through which they trust someone; some people trust easier than others. Most times, those that trust easier than some other people are the ones who fall, victims, more than the other people. Your experience with the perpetrator helped you learn the mechanism you ought to learn towards trusting people. Now, you don't just trust anyone; you will have to be sure people are worth being trusted before you end up trusting them. This is helpful. This perpetrator, with whom you are in a vicious relationship, helped build a good socialization process. This person helped save you from making many mistakes that would have cost you a lot.

From all I have said, you could see that you had long been helpers to each other long before you even started having vicious relation. The both of you have been helping each other even when you don't see each other eye to eye. This triangle of the perpetrator - the victim - helper had long existed between the both of you without acknowledging it. What about imagining how you can, with your positive resources, neutralize your vicious relationship and accept the role of the helper? You have both been helpers even though it took time to realize it; imagine how better things will become now that you have learned it. Everything will go well if both of you agree to embrace forgiveness. Are you finding it difficult to accept forgiveness? Let's go to the next chapter; there is something that I would like to show you there.

Hypnotherapeutic Instruments

Hypnoanalytik

Self Hypnosis

Posthypnotic Suggestion

Active Bridge

Resscourcenorientierte Hypnose

Forgiveness

Power Dialogue:
You Review your Brain

PHS
Post Hypnotic
Suggestions

Regression

Systemtheoretische Hypno Analysis
You Discover Your Multi Face
Personality

Progression

Denseibilisation

My-mindguide.com

Chapter Twelve

THINK LIKE THE PERPETRATOR

Most times, during any disagreement between two people, the person who makes the matter linger even more is the victim. The victim has more possibility of ending the quarrel between them and the perpetrator than the perpetrator has. Let me give a simple example. If a married man was caught cheating on his wife and his wife was so mad at him to the point of filing for divorce, the wife is the victim here while the man is the perpetrator. Looking at the situation, the woman has more power and more inclination to stop the divorce than the man. This man might have been begging for forgiveness and had promised her more than a thousand times that he would never cheat on her again; he had cried, he had called friends to help him out, but his wife stood her ground. After doing all he could to get back his wife, and she remained straight and firmed with her quest for divorce, this man then agreed to go on with it, even though he never wanted it. The divorce process cannot end because the man wanted it to end, remember he did his best even to make sure they didn't consider the divorce, so, if it were in his power to complete the divorce process, he would have done that long time ago, but it is not in his administration. But if this woman who is the victim, who had been the architect of the divorce process, now developed a last-minute change of heart and decided to stop the divorce process, the husband and the wife would get bigger room to get back together.

Let's look at another example; since the advent of Covid-19, burglary had gone a bit up. People now break into people's houses to steal stuff due to how bad the world economy is. Now, let's say someone closed his house and left for work. He usually returns daily from work around the evening time and doesn't return home again after he has gone out for work. Then, this person in his neighborhood had been watching every one of his moves. This person has a strong interest in breaking into this man's house; he intends to steal stuff from this man's house. He continues watching this man closely for a long time. After watching him closely for a long time, he was able to deduce that this man rarely returned home after he had left the house for work. This meant that if he wanted to be successful with his desire to break into the man's house, he would have to do it around when this man was not at home. This burglar then started making accurate plans on how to enter the house; he got his tools ready and waited for the best day and time when he was sure that there would be nobody around in the neighborhood that could see him break into the man's property.

So, one faithful day, this burglar then believes that the correct timing has come. This burglar then gets his tools and, with their help, breaks into this man's house. While he was still searching for what to steal from this man's house, the house owner returned home for the first time in a long time, during the day. He had forgotten something at home and had decided to come to pick it up immediately and return to his place of work. Immediately, the burglar noticed that the owner of the house had returned. He was frustrated; he was destabilized and then started thinking about the quickest measure to take. He already knew that the house owner would find out that the house had been broken on just first glance at the door, which meant more risk for the burglar. The burglar then hides immediately. Immediately the owner of the house came in; he became on high alert; he knew that someone had broken into his house because his door, which he had locked before going out of the house, had been opened. This owner of the house then reached for his gun. This drew more panic for the thief. The thief then indicated his direction and begged for forgiveness. He knew that he could get killed if he didn't act wisely; his only option at that time was to give up on the battle. When he begged for mercy, the owner of the house was now able to know where he was hiding, the owner then walked and stood before him; he pointed his gun at him. Still, he became surprised that the person who had broken into his home was someone from the same neighborhood. He wasn't that close to this person, but they greeted each other whenever they met. This burglar starts begging for mercy, asking the house owner to forgive him.

When we look at the situation of these two people in this room, the burglar broke the door; one is the burglar, the other is the house owner. The burglar is the perpetrator while the house owner is the victim; the burglar is begging and asking the victim, who is the house owner, to pardon him and not involve the police in the incident. The perpetrator here knows that once the police get involved, he will be charged in court, and he will most likely lose the case and get a jail sentence; this was why he was begging for mercy. The victim on his own is now the person to decide whether they would continue to see themselves as victim and perpetrator. In other words, the victim is the one that has to decide whether or not to involve the police. Whatever action that will be taken towards changing the status of their unhealthy relationship is more in the hands of the victim; the perpetrator can beg throughout a whole day. If the victim still refuses to listen to his plea, he would be taken to court. He would be jailed for breaking into someone's house. The perpetrator might have many excuses that he believed pushed him into the action he had taken. He might cite hunger or prolonged unemployment as an excuse, and his reasons could look very reasonable for people to hear, but the final decision on whether to take the case further or drop it rests with the victim. If the victim remains insistent and unforgiving even after all the pleas, the perpetrator will likely be charged to court.

From the examples we cited above, we can see how much power the victim has when it comes to forgiveness when it comes to breaking the vicious relationship between the victim and the perpetrator. We have established that the main person who holds the key to crushing the malicious link between the victim and the perpetrator is the victim.

Some victims will never listen to the perpetrator. Some victims will never consider making peace with the perpetrator on their own. Most times, when you see victims making peace with a perpetrator, it is mainly after a lot of effort from friends and well-wishers. Even at that, the relationship between the victim and the perpetrator still ends up not being very smooth, even if the victim keeps saying he has forgiven the perpetrator. However, the victim keeps showing that he has forgiven the perpetrator, but the truth is that he has yet to forgive the perpetrator. The truth is that he is yet to heal from the pains that the perpetrator caused him.

It is so natural for people offended by what someone has done to them to be myopic in judgment. It's so natural for people who believe that they have been offended only to think one way and not two ways. People who feel offended are sad; they are in pain, and their main focus is that this person who is the perpetrator has done something terrible to them. What this person has done to them bothers them a lot; they hate the fact that this person did this to them. They hate the fact that among all the people in their lives, this is the person whom they trusted with all their heart that ended up doing this to them. The pain is enormous. Because the pain is considerable, it affects the judgment of the victim. It is so difficult to see a victim who is objective in thinking when it comes to discussing why and how they became victims. They are clouded with hate that they can't think objectively when the issue has to do with what happened to them or who did that to them, and you won't blame them considering what was done to them. You won't blame them; they are humans. Humans are bound to think more about themselves than about others.

Now, let's look at the bigger picture. You are indeed the victim; you were indeed the one that was wronged, it is also true that they took advantage of you, but have you ever tried to put yourself in their shoes? Have you ever tried to consider the story they have to tell? You see, one thing about life is that everyone got a story to tell. Everyone got an explanation to give for their action, irrespective of whether their answer is reasonable or not. The fact remains that everyone has something to say to defend their action. Have you ever thought about the motive behind why the perpetrator went ahead to do what they did to you? Have you thought about how reasonable the perpetrator's reason for doing what they did to you is?

Even after careful thinking by the victim, the victim often comes out, feeling indifferent over whatever the perpetrator got to say. The victim has his own story; the victim knew they were on their right. The victim knew that they were the ones who were victimized, so even after listening to the perpetrator's story, most victims still don't feel moved in any way. The question is, why do these victims feel this way? Why do these victims fail to feel moved even after listening to the stories of the perpetrator? This is because the victim has yet to put themself into the perpetrator's shoes to understand what hurt the inner child of the perpetrator so much that made the perpetrator act the way they worked towards the victim.

The truth is that some perpetrators are suffering. I know that it isn't every perpetrator that is suffering, but some are suffering, and when they try to voice out their suffering, they end up making a victim of the person they love most. There was this man that constantly abused his wife verbally and mentally. He wasn't always like this. His wife had been with him for a long time, and according to her, he was the best man she could ever ask for; she couldn't understand why their relationship turned out the way it did. For months and a year, this woman kept thinking about why her husband acted this way. This husband was also talking to himself sometimes; he wasn't always happy after realizing how badly he was treating his wife. He didn't like what was happening; he wanted to make a change, but he found himself still behaving the same way most times. At some point, it became a big issue. The wife was already starting to have enough of it and thought of divorce. Someone brought the idea of them going for a therapy session. It was their last hope of salvaging the situation. During this session, it was discovered that this man was very hurt; he was significantly damaged because of how his wife was raped. He knew it wasn't her fault, but he didn't understand why he kept taking it out on her, even when he had promised himself that he was going to stop. Even after his wife found her ways to put the trauma she went through into check, this man had his depression eating him up. He was suffering. He was battling with something, and you would have to put yourself in his shoes; you would have to think like him to understand the gravity of what he was battling. His inner child was hurt so much; he didn't know how to heal it, he didn't know how to go about it, he just found himself hurting the woman he loved over something that was in no way her fault. This man might have been instrumental in helping her heal from the trauma she suffered from the rape; he might have been one of her most robust support systems who assisted her to break out from the circle of the trauma she was going through. Despite all this, his inner child was hurt, battling with many things, and everything came out from the way he abused his wife.

Suppose you can bring yourself into imagining the real reason behind the perpetrator's action. In that case, if you can get yourself into the perpetrator's shoes, it will help you understand the perpetrator more. It will help you make up your inner mind on the act of forgiving the perpetrator. As I already said, forgiveness is more of what is perceived or felt than what is articulated or what action or inactions were taken. It has to start from the heart for it to be absolute forgiveness. Until you understand why the perpetrator did what they did, you might not be able to perceive or feel it in your heart to forgive the perpetrator; you may continue to hurt in your heart.

The Drama Triangle (Forgive The Past)

Neighbors

Helper
(Person and Neighbor)

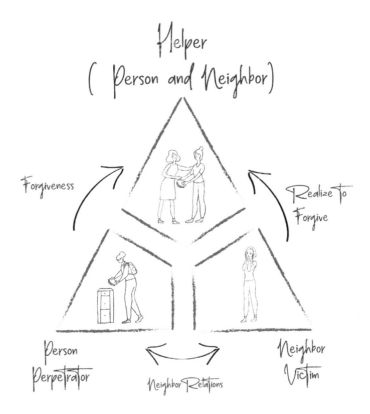

Forgiveness

Realize To Forgive

Person Perpetrator

Neighbor Relations

Neighbor Victim

Chapter Thirteen

WHY WE SHOULD ESCAPE THE VICIOUS CIRCLE

When I was younger, I used to be part of this group of friends. We always hung out from time to time and spent a lot of fun time together. Being together was fun because we made ourselves happy. We all watched each other's back and helped each other when one of us was in need or in a particular situation that needed our attention. So, there were these two among us who always had issues. One was a boy and the other a girl. The boy always found it difficult to tolerate the girl, and the girl always found faults in whatever the boy was doing. They always had issues, but because we were always in the company of each other, they always found a way to settle their issues. So, it got to the point that these two had an issue; this issue was so severe that it lasted longer than the other issues they had before. We became worried and tried our ways to settle the issue for them, but the girl stood her ground and said she didn't want anything to do with the guy again. The guy didn't stress it; he just acted cool as if it wasn't a big deal. There was this side hustle this guy was doing at the time to get a little cash for himself. So, one day he went to this side hustle with another guy that was part of our group. They mostly do this hustle together.

While they were doing this, this guy who had an issue with this girl was involved in a car accident. He died from the wounds he sustained from this car accident. We were crushed. He was so young, but death couldn't spare him. We all cried, but I noticed something. This girl who refused to make peace with him cried maybe twenty times more than we did. She regretted not being able to forgive him to her bone marrow. This made her hate herself. Sometimes, an intense regret comes from refusing to break out from the vicious circle you are keeping with someone you had refused to forgive. It hits you so hard when the guilt comes that you even get depressed from it. You can imagine that this guy's mom even had to console her because she saw how badly she was affected. It was very massive on her. The vicious circle often leads to regret. It usually leaves you so heartbroken; it often leaves you wishing you have broken out from it. This starts surfacing after it has caused different series of harm to you.

There are a lot of reasons why you should break out from the vicious circle. I would like to talk about some of these reasons:

1. Breaking out from the vicious circle sets you free. As much as you will refuse to accept this, the truth is that the vicious circle you have trapped yourself in is like a prison. You can become confined to this circle like a prisoner. You don't get the freedom your heart requires. Whenever the person you are trapped with in this circle comes to mind, you get into

trouble. You start wishing many things; some might even begin to curse at nobody's insight. It affects you mentally. You become a victim of mental slavery. The time you should have used to think about productive stuff, you waste that time thinking about the person with whom you are trapped in the vicious circle. Putting yourself together and making up your mind to break out from this circle will set you free. There are no two ways about this. There is no way around it; if you want to be free, you will have to work for your freedom, and you will have to set yourself free. You will have to break the vicious circle.

2. It helps you move forward with your life. Imagine someone being trapped in a painful past for a long time; that person continues going around a circle like a dot in a circle who can never go out of the process. This is how it is for people who trap themselves in the vicious circle. You can't move forward. Your life will still be in the past; you will be living your present in your history. You will end up hurting other people around you because of your past. This can make you someone that everybody around you will be seeing as a miserable or troublesome person.

People who know you will avoid doing things with you because they know you could end up hurting them. If you want to move forward with your life, you have to break out of that vicious circle. You have to eliminate that circle. You have to forgive that person you believe is the perpetrator; you have to heal from those unseen wounds which are beginning to affect your life negatively. You have to move on with your life. For you to do this, break out from the vicious circle.

3. It begins your healing process: the only reason why you are still filled with hate for the perpetrator is that you are yet to heal from what you believe the perpetrator had done to you. You are yet to let go of the pains of what you think the perpetrator did. In other words, even though it's been a long time since you had this experience that had locked you up in a vicious circle, you are yet to begin your healing process; you are yet to start healing. There is no way you can recover from your past if you fail to break out from the vicious circle that this past had entrapped you in. There is no way you can become a better person if you can't heal from this past that is now haunting you. There is no way you will get through happiness if you can't get true healing from this very past. Your true healing begins when you find the will and the zeal to break out from the vicious circle. Only after you make up your mind to break from this vicious circle will you be able to access your complete healing.

4. Breaking out from this vicious circle helps remove the anger that had built up in your heart over the years—having continuous irritation that surfaces from time to time causes those who find themselves caught up in this anger to transfer their aggression to someone else that has not a single thing to do with their anger. Breaking out from this vicious circle doesn't just set you free from accumulated anger; it also frees you from malice. People who harbor malice are potential criminals; they may end up doing things that they will regret for the rest of their lives, things that could ruin the perpetrator and themselves as the victim. Malice is often the bedrock of many crimes happening in

different places. When people feel they have been wronged or cheated, malice comes in. It is okay for malice to come in for just a short while, but it is a problem when it comes in and remains there without leaving. This malice and anger make the victim lose their sense of empathy; the only thing that will be crossing their heart is how to harm the perpetrator, get back at the perpetrator, or pay back the perpetrator for what the perpetrator had done to them. You have to break out of this vicious circle now to get rid of anger and malice. The longer they accumulate, the more dangerous they become for you. This is because they may end up robbing you of your proper sense of judgment and end up taking away your good heart and replacing it with a heart of chaos.

5. When you break out of this vicious circle, you no longer give someone control over your mind. As logical as it may sound, the truth is that some people have lost control over their life. There are so many people out there who are not in control of their lives or their judgment. Their life is like someone addicted to drugs. When people use drugs, they take actions very much contrary to the effort they would have taken when they were in their right state of mind. Some of them go out and attack people they wouldn't have attacked if they were in their right state of mind; some even go as far as getting someone killed in the process. When they were doing all these, they were not in control of their emotions; they were not in control of what was going on in their minds; everything about them was controlled by the drugs they were high on. In the end, they end up committing crimes that would put them behind bars for many years;

they end up committing crimes that could take away their "right to life." They couldn't get hold of themselves when they committed this crime, but they are still going to suffer severely for it. This is synonymous with someone who is trapped in a vicious circle. When you are trapped in a vicious circle, you are not in control of your mind; you are not in control of your life. The hate you have for the victim or the perpetrator is in control of your life. The hatred you have for the perpetrator will be the thing that discerns the actions you take. You might start acting wicked; you might become callous; you might become a cheat; you might become an abuser of any kind; all these and many more are very unpleasant things you will be known for. Most of the things you do will be moving in the direction that shows that you are acting due to what you have accumulated in your heart. You are not in control of your life if you are trapped in a vicious circle. The circle controls you. All the hate packed in your heart that makes you remain like a prisoner in this circle will keep coming out in different ways and affecting your life in different ways. You will end up being a terrible person. You will have no joy. What others do and find happiness from, you wouldn't be capable; why? Because you are trapped in a vicious circle. Break out from this circle. Own your life. Own yourself.

6. Breaking out from this vicious circle also mentally helps heal the perpetrator. The truth is that not every perpetrator is terrible in every way. As we already stressed out in some of the stories above, we saw that people ended up hurting other people because they were hurt. The perpetrator might be going through stuff when they broke you; you might

have even been the one that hurt this perpetrator that eventually turned you into their victim. After your perpetrator hurt you, they released that what they have done to you was wrong in every ramification; they also became a victim. They start suffering from the very fact that they are the cause of your pain; they start suffering for the fact that they were the ones that made your life as miserable as it turned out. Even when they manage to forget what they had done to you for a short while, they keep seeing things that remind them of what they had done to you. Even after they had been able to withstand the torment they face from seeing things that remind them of what they did to you, whenever they lay their eyes on you, they can become miserable, and even more tormented. The guilt tries to kill them. This can go a long way to affect the perpetrator mentally. So, breaking out from the vicious circle will not only be freeing you, but it will also be freeing your perpetrator. Perhaps you still wish not to see your perpetrator free in any way; remember that you are locking yourself up as you continue to lock your perpetrator. While your perpetrator is a prisoner to you, you are a prisoner to the vicious circle and indirectly a prisoner to your perpetrator. You have to break out from the vicious circle to free yourself and every other person caught in the vicious circle. Fix your mental health and fix the person's mental health that made you a victim.

7. Do you know that forgiveness is the best revenge you can give? Listen to this; the law of gravity says that whatever goes up must surely make its way back to the ground, especially when this is happening on the earth. If you throw

a stone into the air, you will see the stone coming back to you. Some forces want you to remain in this vicious circle. These forces want you to become or stay a terrible person. They have trapped you down in a vicious circle for too long; they are doing this to change you for the worse; in fact, they have caused a lot of damage to you. You have to get your revenge. This time around, your perpetrator may not be the one you are taking your revenge on; your payback will be against those forces trying to pull you down. Your revenge will be against that vicious circle. You have to take your revenge on that vicious circle for trapping you inside it for too long. Break out from it, get your sweet revenge.

Chapter Fourteen

SELF-FORGIVENESS

I have been talking about forgiveness in several chapters already, but I haven't really talked deeply about self-forgiveness, so here we are now.

Self-forgiveness entails forgiving yourself for that very thing you believe you shouldn't have done, which you nonetheless did. You forgive yourself for that regrettable stuff for which you keep blaming yourself. You decide to free yourself from the misery in which you have caged yourself due to how much you hated yourself for doing something or not doing something. The worst form of pain one will ever be subjected to is intrinsic misery. I am not saying external hell is not as miserable, but innate despair is on another level when it comes to being sad or catastrophic. When people suffer from external misery or misery that has to do with their environment, they get relief when they leave their environment somewhere else. When people have an outward affliction linked to the people they see, it is superficial; the people they see are part of their environment. When they don't see these particular people, they start feeling better or escape for a moment or an extended moment from their misery; these are all irrelevant forms of torture. But when the pain is intrinsic, the discomfort resides within the person; this person goes about their daily activities with this misery going about with them. These people continue to fight battles that are within, they can get exhausted from what is happening within them.

People are battling with a problem or mistake they made in the past, for which they ought to forgive themselves to fight a lot of intrinsic battles. They hate themselves; they hate that same experience that made them hate themselves. They do their best to kick the memory of what happened out of their mind, but it doesn't work out for them the way they wanted. Why? Because they are doing it the wrong way, perhaps because they have not made up their minds to forgive themselves.

What happened that made you start feeling this guilt that has been with you for a long time that you just can't rid of your life? Do you know that what happened might not be your fault if it was your fault? Do you know that you feel terrible about it, the fact that you get bothered a lot about it, even after it's been a long time since it happened, showed that you have a good heart?

You are human, after all. Humans are not known to be perfect. If a man comes out and says something to everybody in his country, and no one has anything ill to say about it, then there might be a problem. There must be criticism. People will always find faults in what he said or from some of the stuff he said to them. The only perfect person on earth is a madman. A madman sees himself right in everything he says and does, and those around him watching never say anything to counter the madman because they know the madman is mad. The madman looks right and perfect in all he says because those around him ignored him after considering that he somewhat had dementia. So, if no man out there is perfect, why should you be perfect? If no man is above making mistakes, why should you hold on to a mistake you made over years ago and allow yourself to be tied like a rope by this mistake? Mistakes are meant to be made. Errors are typical for humans to make them. Ask any prominent businessman out there who had succeeded in managing a company for a long time; you will end up seeing from their confessions that they had made countless mistakes since the establishment. Even though they look big today, even though they look too good today, it doesn't erase the fact that they made many mistakes in the past while trying to grow their businesses. The absence of errors doesn't in any way discern perfection; the lack of errors may rather mean that someone is pretending to be what they are not or putting out a fake life or a fake story. The presence of mistakes shows you are human. It shows that you are not suffering from mental issues; you are not perfect.

Great men make mistakes countless times, but when they do, they do their best not to make the same mistakes again. They make sure they learn the lesson they are meant to learn from their mistakes. After learning this lesson, they become even better and more significant in life. It is inappropriate to continue dwelling on the errors when one makes mistakes. It is one thing to make mistakes and remain in the shadow of your mistakes; it is another thing to make a mistake and refuse to dwell on the errors, thereby going all out to get things done in better ways than before. Because they already had experience from their past mistakes, they never repeated them.

Now, let's say you made a mistake, something you feel badly about. That was a mistake you made. It is okay to mourn over your mistakes, but the question is, how long will you mourn? How long will you continue to keep yourself confined to that same mistake you made? Does mourning and stressing yourself out over the error you made change the fact that you made that mistake? No! All the years you wasted mourning over your errors and hating yourself for it should have been used to move farther in life; it should have been used to correct your mistake and become even better than you are now. You have to forgive yourself. You have to let yourself heal from the pain that had been inflicted on you by that same mistake you made.

The road to self-forgiveness is the purposeful way that often transforms people into their best version. The version they have failed to be over the months or years they had been mourning over their mistakes. There are several steps to take towards achieving self-forgiveness; let's look at some of them:

1. Make up your mind: the first-ever step towards forgiving yourself for whatever that had been troubling you is to accept that you want to forgive yourself. You have to accept that you have mourned enough over this particular mistake. You have to accept that you have been wasting your time grieving over this specific mistake. You have to make up your mind that enough is enough. You have to make up your mind that you want a change. Change is the only

constant thing in life, but most times, if you want to change your life, especially when the change you want to generate is positive, you have to work for it. You have to put in a lot of work. You can't bring change into your state of holding on to your mistakes unless you are willing to work to effect a change. For you to be ready to put up with the challenging work, you should at least have made up your mind for it. Bad habits are not easy to drop; to drop a bad habit, it must involve some fight. It has to affect the willingness to forego certain things that wouldn't help you in your quest to drop that bad habit. You have been mourning over your mistakes for too long; you have been blaming yourself for your mistake for too long; it has found a way to become part of you. It is trying to ruin you and prevent you from going far in life; you have to make up your mind to fight back and kick it out of your heart.

2. Understand your emotions: Understanding the emotions that have been hitting you badly is one of the first steps you must take if you are serious about forgiving yourself for whatever mistake you believe you made in the past. Certain emotions always come in to put you out; those emotions always make their way to your heart, and they cast guilt on you whenever they do that. You have to understand these emotions; you must know that they are there to disorganize and destabilize you. When you know them and the pattern they use to get at you, you will now know how to overcome them.

3. Stop the blame game: you can't be able to forgive yourself if you are still bent on blaming yourself for what happened.

Yes, it is good to take responsibility; in fact, taking responsibility for your actions shows your great sense of maturity, but the time of mourning is over. You have mourned over your actions for too long. The world will never remain at a point just because you are grieving over the mistake you made. The world wouldn't come to sympathize with you after you continue losing all that you are meant to gain because you are holding onto a past mistake that you made. You have to stop blaming yourself. Yes, it happened, and there is nothing that you can do about it. I know you might be wishing you had done something differently; perhaps you believe it would have changed the outcome. The truth is that if it is meant to happen, you wouldn't possibly be able to change the product. It happened because it was meant to happen, and since it already happened, you can't change the fact that it happened. Blaming yourself will only make you continue to wallow in bitterness. Bitter people don't move ahead in life. Upset people don't attract opportunities; you can do better.

4. Think of your mistake as a lesson: if people can come to terms with seeing the task their mistakes show them, a lot of people would have made it bigger in their lives. The strong learn from their mistakes; they don't remain mourning over their mistakes for too long. We always hear people say that experience is the best teacher. What that means is that, after having a specific incident that makes you uncomfortable, you can figure how to prevent the same experience from happening again. After making a mistake, you are meant to learn from that mistake; you are meant to adapt your life better in a way that such a mistake will not win over the

next time that it surfaces. You are meant to learn from your experience how that mistake was able to win you; these will help you know how not to make the same mistake again. You didn't make that mistake for you to continue mourning over the mistake for the rest of your life. That a mistake was made never meant that your life is over. That you made just one mistake, whether small or big, doesn't mean that you are done. Let's look at an artist's work; drawing an image doesn't clean the whole drawing after making just one mistake. The artist does erase the mistake and looks for how to make it better; while he is looking for how to improve it, he will make sure he doesn't make the same mistake again. Compare yourself to this artist. If the artist stops drawing and continues wasting his time complaining about the mistake, he wouldn't finish the drawing. If you continue to mourn over that mistake which you are yet to forgive yourself for doing, you may end up being a mistake. Yes, your entire self might end up being a mistake. This is something that will look too degrading. So, make sure you see your mistake as your lesson, stop seeing your mistake as your cross, stop seeing it as your problem, stop seeing it as your burden, see it as your teacher.

5. Fight the replay: one of the main reasons why it seems you can't get over the thought of the mistake haunting you is that everything keeps replaying itself in your head. You keep getting reminded of what you did; you keep getting reminded of what you should have done, which you didn't do. Everything keeps replaying, and you find all the bad moods and emotions getting their stronghold on you. You can't stop yourself from having a particular thought about

something, you can't stop an image from appearing in your memory, you can't stop a video from playing in your brain, but there is this thing that you can do. You can stop yourself from dwelling on a thought. When an idea comes in, it is left for you to decide on whether to analyze this thought or face it out. You can prevent yourself from expanding a study that just came into your mind. When an image comes into your memory, you can block your brain from continuously viewing that image. In other words, after just a glance, the brain stops a continuous glimpse of the image in your memory. When a video comes in, you can also block your brain from watching the content of this video. Thoughts, photos, and videos that show you your mistakes are one of the main reasons you can't get them off your mind. You may not be able to stop them from coming whenever they feel like coming, but you can stop yourself from exploring them. When this continues for a long time, these thoughts, images, and videos will disappear even without you knowing when or how. If you want to forgive yourself, you must be ready to fight the replay; it will do you no good at the moment.

6. Seek therapy: you may need to seek treatment depending on the kind of damage your continuous dwelling in your mistakes had done on you. Some people dwelling on their past and having issues forgiving themselves suffer from a very stubborn depression. Some of them are at the state that they now believe they don't deserve to be alive. They are already considering suicide because they think they deserve to die for what they did. Therapy will be beneficial in helping you wrangle your depression. After controlling the cause of

your depression and then handling the depression, you will come out a better person.

Before I conclude this chapter, I would like to say that self-forgiveness is very therapeutical. It heals your inner child.

No matter how deeply your mistakes have condemned you, self-forgiveness will erase all the condemnation. To forgive yourself, you will have to make up your mind; you will have to decide to let go. It may not be something that you will achieve overnight, but you will get there with more work.

The Ritual

Power Circle — Imagined

3X
Breathout

5X
Move Arms

My-mindguide.com

Chapter Fifteen

I CAN EVEN FORGIVE MY TENANT

If there is anything I am so proud of, it is the fact that I was able to own property. It takes a lot of hard work to save money and buy property. It is one thing to be making a lot of money; it is another to keep the money you make and use it for the suitable investment when the opportunity arrives. Some people have made a lot of money in their life, but they have nothing to show for it. They have no savings of their own, and they surprisingly didn't have any investment they had made for themselves. Money is just like a baby; when you give birth to a baby, the baby's well-being depends on you. The baby is still tiny and can't fend for themself. The baby depends solely on you. If you take care of the baby the best way you know you ought to, the baby will grow well and look very healthy. If you don't take care of the baby the way you should, the baby will look dirty and malnourished; in worst cases, the baby might even die from the lack of care they are getting from you. When you compare this with money, you will see a significant similarity. Money is like a baby; when you take care of your money, save as much as you ought to save, spend wisely, invest wisely, your money will keep growing. If you don't take care of your money the way you ought to, by spending extravagantly, not saving, and making unrealistic investments, you will go broke before you know what is happening. You will end up losing all the money you have because you didn't take care of your money the way you ought to have taken care of it. So many people became broke from missing this ideology. No money spent is ever coming back. This is why it is always advisable to pay less than what you earn. This is why it is always advisable to put your money into something that will bring you more money, something that is legal and, at the same time, productive.

So, I decided to invest my money in getting a property after I had saved for a very long time. I got this property that I loved so much, but with my mindset that was very much set on business, I decided that I would rent out my property. I knew it would bring me a lot of money every year. I was excited that I was now a landlord. The feeling was incredible; it was even more remarkable as I became aware of the reality that I would be getting a lot of money for rent—renting a big house like the property I have would cost a fortune. Whoever was going to live there would be better off financially. So, I needed a tenant to come in and stay in my house. Before then, I had heard of how problematic some tenants could be. Some tenants will make you regret ever owning a home. I listened to a lot of stuff, but I didn't want to be pessimistic about my joy because I was now a landlord who owned property. I knew there were so many good tenants out there; I didn't see the need to wish myself a lousy tenant on a property I had just acquired. So, I got a tenant. This tenant seemed so calm. After the experience I had with this tenant, I realized that the quiet people are always the ones you should watch out for; they are the ones who would stab you when you least expect and where it would pain you the most.

So, this tenant moved in. I didn't suspect anything fishy about this tenant because he looked calm and responsible. As time went on, I started seeing the part of this tenant which I never noticed. He refused to pay the rent he owed us. I didn't know the motive behind this, but he refused to pay. He invented damages as a cause of not paying. As he was also a lawyer, he was very creative. Long lists – this absolute to highest standard built luxury mansion should be a barrack? Everything was strange. I didn't understand why someone could start acting that way out of nowhere. It was just like the case of two people who never argued, two people who never quarreled with each other, and they started having physical combat. Everything was just so surprising and strange. So, the court decided to ask a sworn appraiser to check the existence of all the damages. Out of a list of 132 so-called damages, he determined 0 factual damages. After hard-fought battles in the courts, revisions he had to leave, he lost his lawyer licence and had to deliver an oath of disclosure. Sad also for his family and his two little kids.

I tried to understand why this man did what he did; I concluded that maybe he did because he couldn't pay the rent he owed us. It would be against the contract if he didn't pay, but I would have preferred him to contact me and tell me that he was having trouble paying the rent. I would have understood his situation, and maybe I would have given him more time, but he tried to play me. I forgave him anyway.

The Conclusion

I n conclusion, there is power in forgiveness. Forgiving people for what they have done to you might not be as easy as it sounds, but it is one of the highest forms of courage one will ever take. Forgiving yourself for whatever mistake you believe you have made is as vital as whatever top priority you have in life. People who don't forgive can't have peace of mind, or learn from their mistakes. They will remain controlled by their hate. And above all, people who can't forgive can't heal.

The journey for me was to learn to look deeper, and I wanted to free myself from the role of being a victim or even sometimes a perpetrator. Today, I see in a Perpetrator always the little child, hurt and craving for love and attention. I see the deeper cause for bad behavior. The deed I can't forgive. Because a bad deed stays, I distinguish between deed and perpetrator.

If you enjoyed this title and would like to read about other topics that have changed my life, please check out my new books on Amazon or my website:

www.my-mindguide.com.

Also, let's stay connected on social media. Please drop a line on Facebook or Instagram, and stay tuned for updates! You're welcome to share your thoughts with me directly as well: gassner@my-mindguide.com. In return, I'll send you a gorgeous infographic that you can cut out and frame.

Also, please leave a review on Amazon, as this will help me to reach an even broader audience. Thank you so much for your time, insight, and undying hunger for knowledge!

I want to say thank you to all of my colleagues, clients, friends, and family members, who have all contributed to what I am now.

I also want to say thank you to Gabriel Palacios, the king of hypnotherapy and a Swiss bestseller author who taught this old fox new tricks, letting me deep-dive into the mystery of hypnotherapy. I learned so much along the journey that I'm now a certified master-hypnosis coach and conversation coach myself!

Furthermore, I want to say thank you to the fantastic teachers of SAMYANA/Bali who trained me to become a certified yoga and meditation teacher. &&&

Last but not least, I give a special thanks to my master-teacher Eckhard Wunderle, who's close to a saint to me. He introduced me to the world of meditation and let me discover all the wonders it has to offer. I couldn't be more proud about having received my certification as a meditation teacher from directly from him at the Institut für Spirituelle Psychologie.

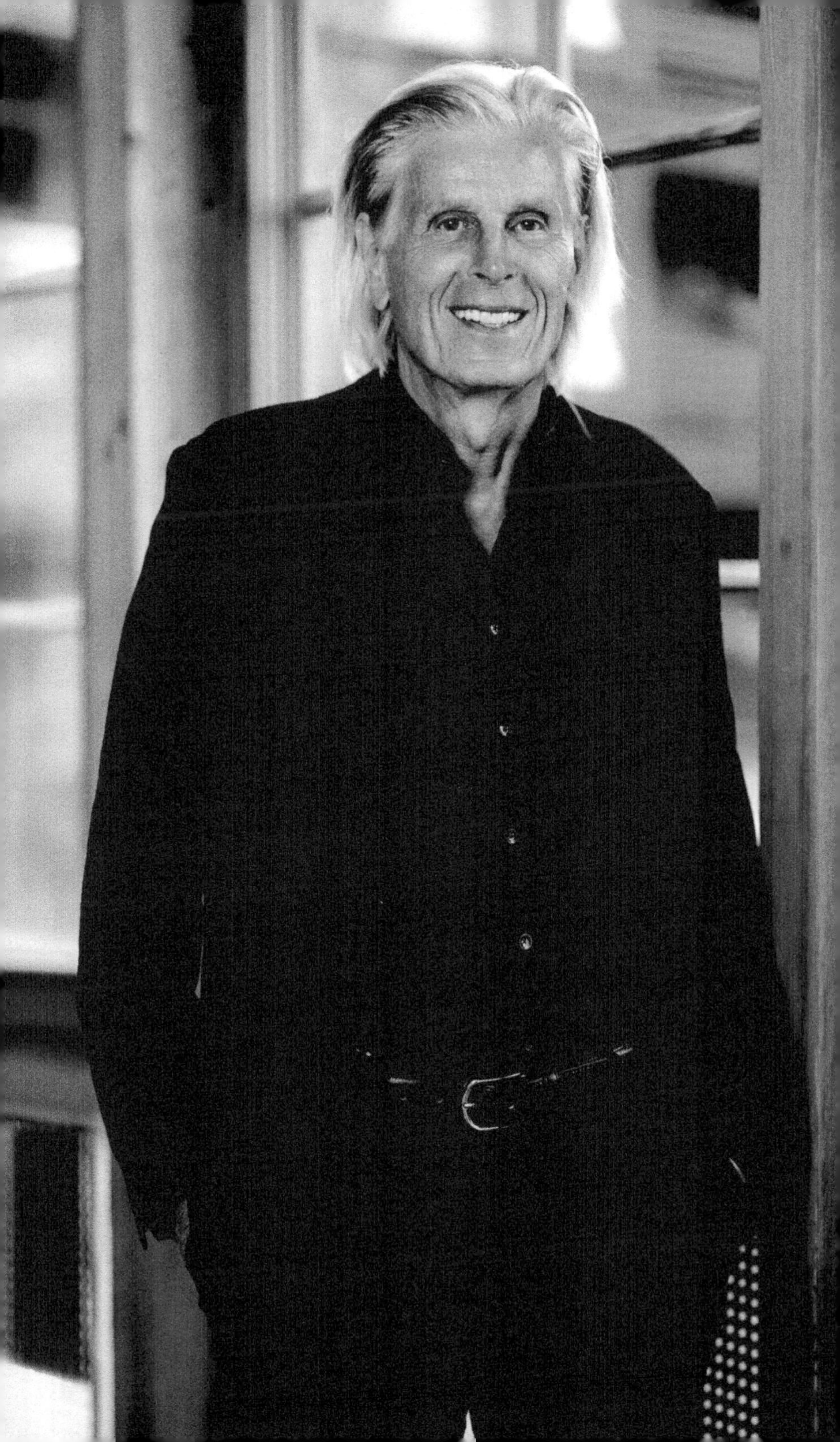

Authors Bio

Kurt Friedrich Gassner has worn many hats throughout his lifetime, including but not limited to serial entrepreneur, creative director, meditation teacher, licensed hypnotherapist, and more recently, self-improvement author. Leveraging his treasure trove of experiences and in-depth knowledge of psychology, he provides his readers with the tools they need to unlock their infinite potential.

As a prolific self-help writer, Kurt has authored the following books: *The Art of Forgiveness, Lie or Die, Soul-Match, Can You Inherit a Poisoned Mind?* and *The Power of Poverty*. He also authored a best-selling children's book in German-speaking countries and has over twenty books underway.

When it comes to enduring success, Kurt understands that financial prosperity isn't the only aspect one should strive for. He may be a self-made millionaire, but what really transformed his life is mastering his unconscious mind. Perseverance, personal power, self-awareness, and learning from past mistakes have all been key ingredients to bringing his dreams to fruition—and he strives to impart that wisdom to others through his writing.

In his spare time, Kurt Friedrich Gassner is either traveling across the globe, golfing, biking in the Alps, hiking, or spending quality time with his loved ones. For the last thirty-seven years, he has been happily married and he is the father of two successful children. Presently, he resides in both Munich, Germany, and Kirchberg, Austria.

Series
FORGIVNESS TODAY

POWER & ART OF FORGIVNESS

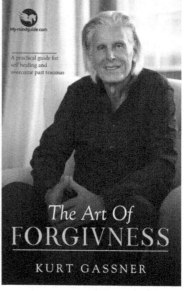

UPCOMING BOOKS BY THE AUTHOR

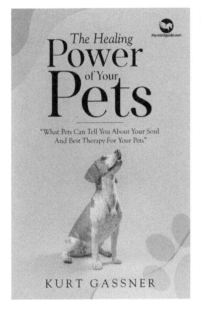

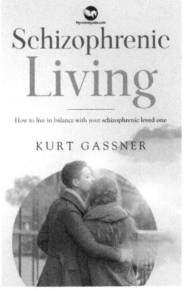